D0622899

DISCARDED

Women's Rights in International Documents

To Marjorie and
the other women
of the world

Women's Rights in International Documents

A Sourcebook with Commentary

by
Winston E. Langley

McFarland & Company, Inc., Publishers
Jefferson, North Carolina, and London

ADM 8482

British Library Cataloguing-in-Publication data are available

Library of Congress Cataloguing-in-Publication Data

Langley, Winston.
    Women's rights in international documents : a sourcebook
with commentary / by Winston E. Langley.
        p. cm.
    Includes bibliographical references and index.
    ISBN 0-89950-548-1 (lib. bdg. : 50# alk. paper) ∞
    1. Women—Legal status, laws, etc. 2. Women's rights. I. Title.
K644.L36 1991
346.01'34—dc20
[342.6134]
                                                                                90-53501
                                                                                CIP

Manufactured in the United States of America

McFarland & Company, Inc., Publishers
    Box 611, Jefferson, North Carolina 28640

Table of Contents

Preface

The conviction which urged the preparation of this volume is that insufficient attention has been given to the efforts of the international community to advance the rights of women. In particular, it is the view of the writer that, except for *Women's Legal Rights* by Malvina Halberstam and Elizabeth Defeis—a book that focuses on international covenants as an alternative to the Equal Rights Amendment in the U.S.—few works have acknowledged the potential contributions of internationally recognized instruments that establish rights for women. These instruments seek to reform national as well as international processes and structures that define and promote gender discrimination. Indeed, many persons involved in the struggle for gender equality have little or no knowledge of those rights.

It is the principal aim of this book to serve as a documentary source for the important international instruments that deal with the rights of women. A secondary aim is to provide a context for and a perspective on the documents, in order to help readers begin to make preliminary assessments or at least encourage them to think further about some of the issues associated with the internationally recognized rights.

Finally, I want to thank the International Legal Studies Library at Harvard University, the Boston University Law School Library, the Women's Studies Library at the Massachusetts Institute of Technology, and the staff of the Healey Library at the University of Massachusetts at Boston for the assistance they gave me during the preparation of this work.

Introduction

The term "women's rights," as used in this work, denotes those areas of human rights which have evolved since World War II to express the global community's commitment to the outlawing of sex-based discrimination. In an affirmative vein, those rights are also seen as part of an effort to promote the general norm of non-discrimination.

Since human rights are, by nature, applicable to "all persons," "every human being," and "all members of the human family," women are, by definition, individually and collectively accorded protection under relevant regional and global human rights instruments. Logically, therefore, there should be no need for a separate grouping of rights for women.

Women, however, suffer from historic deprivations—deprivations that have no bearing either on their social contributions or their capabilities—that show disregard for rights recognized as inhering to *everyone*. Accordingly, the international community concluded that it was both just and proper to create certain human rights instruments (or portions of them) that bear uniquely on women.

The documents which follow represent the major areas on which the global community, principally through the U.N. system, has sought to focus its efforts to outlaw sexual discrimination. Here a brief summary of their thrust will be given as well as an identification of the U.N. organs which have had the most direct responsibility for their elaboration and adoption. Specific comments will then precede each document.

The U.N. Organs

The United Nations has six principal organs—the Security Council, the Trusteeship Council, the International Court of Justice, the Secretariat, the General Assembly, and the Economic and Social Council (ECOSOC). While all six, to some degree, have some relationship with human rights in general, and woman's rights in particular, the latter three organs are the ones with which we will be primarily concerned, because they are the ones chiefly involved in the development and implementation of the rights under discussion. (We will also have occasion to mention the U.N. Educational, Scientific and Cultural Organizations and the International Labor Organization—the ILO.)

In case of the Secretariat, which is the chief administrative organ of the United Nations, as will subsequently be seen, its role has varied from that of recommending or encouraging the initiation of studies and the organizing and supporting of conferences, to the marshaling of evidence and the shaping of political support. The General Assembly, on the other hand, is the organ which has the ultimate say as regards whether particular moral entitlements or claims are adopted as rights and then recommended to states for ratification. It is only after the latter process that such claims become an international right binding on states.

Finally, the ECOSOC is perhaps the organ that is most centrally involved in the field of human rights, and it has—as a subsidiary body—the U.N. Commission on the Status of Women (the Commission or CSW), which was established in 1947. That commission is the only international intergovernmental body responsibile for preparing recommendations and reports pursuant to the promotion of women's rights in political, social and cultural fields. The CSW also makes recommendations to the Economic and Social Council on problems viewed as requiring immediate attention in the field of women's rights, especially as that attention may contribute to the furthering of the principle that men and women should have equal rights.

Summary of Rights

Although there are many ways to group the rights covered in the documents to follow, any discussion or study of those rights may be made easier if they were organized into the two subclasses with which they are commonly identified: (a) the civil and political; and (b) the economic, social and cultural. We will, therefore, observe this classification in our summary, discussing first the civil and political.

Apart from recognizing that women enjoy rights in civil matters identical to that of men—for instance, the right to a fair trial and to a life of freedom of conscience and expression—the relevant international instruments under consideration have highlighted other rights such as the right to vote in all elections and to be eligible for election to *all* publicly elected bodies; to participate in the formulation of government policy and the implementation thereof; and to take part in nongovernmental organizations and associations concerned with the public life of nation-states. These nation-states pledge to take "all appropriate measures" to ensure that women, on equal terms with men and without discrimination, have the opportunity to represent their governments at the international level and participate in the work of international organizations.

Part of civil and political rights (as well as economic, social and cultural) is the right to a nationality. International legal instruments impose a duty on states to recognize women as having, on equal terms with men, the right to acquire, change or retain their nationality; and further, to ensure that neither marriage to an alien nor change of nationality by the husband during the marriage shall automatically modify the nationality of the wife, render her stateless, or force upon her the nationality of her husband. States are also enjoined to grant women equal rights with men in respect of the nationality of their children.

Framers of the human rights instruments understood that women would have to take an active role in fashioning the equality they should enjoy and that women's political empowerment would be an indispensable instrumental goal on the social road to equality. Therefore one should understand "the right to vote in all elections," to be "eligible for election to publicly elected bodies," and to "hold public office and exercise *all* public functions." It is within that context, too, that one should see the emphasis on women's right to participate in public life at the international, national, local and community levels. On the international level there was a time when women were rarely, if ever participants in diplomatic, consular, administrative and judicial activities. Today, even in case of the more "enlightened states," only a few are represented. But as the policies at the international level increasingly shape what takes place nationally and locally—especially in the area of political economy—the equal presence of women in international councils will be correspondingly important. The linking of the right to vote with the right to actually formulate and implement public policy reflects the realization that, even in societies where the major features of patriarchy have been seriously questioned and challenged, the right to vote by and of itself can be a mere formality, contributing little or nothing to the goal of sexual equality.

As before indicated, one of the rights with which the global community has been concerned in relationship to women is that of nationality. States, by law, had (some still do) required that a woman who married an alien (a citizen or national of a state other than that of which the woman is a citizen) would automatically lose her former nationality and gain that of her husband. Should this marriage be subsequently dissolved, she could then lose her newly-gained nationality and, thereby, become a stateless person, with the loss of all the international protection that this status entails. The justification for this leaguing of the wife's nationality to that of her husband's was the traditional principle of unity of the family, but that unity, where it existed, was purchased at the price of, and clearly reflected, the social inequality of women.

The Convention on the Elimination of All Forms of Discrimination Against Women (CEDAW), in its elaboration of the right of women to acquire, retain, or change their nationality as they choose, represents the culmination of efforts since the 1930s to change the traditional law relating to nationality and replace it with the principle of independence and equality of women. Family unity on this basis is the only type worth supporting.[1]

The subclass of rights which we above characterized as economic, social and cultural, deal with matters relating to employment, economic and social order, education, health care, marriage, and the family. The international instruments which espouse this category of rights employ as their major premise the view that genuine equality between women and men can be brought about only if nobody is forced into predetermined roles on acount of sex.

Regarding the areas of employment, nation-states assume the obligation to eliminate discrimination against women and ensure equality with men. In particular, states pledge to recognize women as having the same right as men to employment opportunities, to the free choice of profession and employment, to promotion and job security, to receive vocational training, to *equal remuneration* and treatment with respect *to work of equal value,* and to obtain social security as well as employment and disability benefits. Women are also recognized to have a right to "protection of health and safety, in working conditions, including safeguarding of the function of reproduction."[2]

Human rights instruments seek to prevent the discrimination against women "on the grounds of marriage or maternity." So, in order to "ensure them the *effective right to work,*"[3] these states assume the obligation to take measures to "prohibit discrimination" against women on grounds of pregnancy, maternity leave or marital status. Nation-states further pledge themselves to introduce maternity leave with pay or comparable social benefits without loss of former employment seniority or social allowances and to encourage the development of supporting social services that are necessary to enable parents to combine family responsibilities with work obligations. States vow to eliminate discrimination against women in the exercise of their right to family benefits, bank loans, mortgages, and other forms of financial credit.[4] (One should note here that special provisions are made for women in rural areas.)

In the area of health, women are recognized to enjoy the right to "appropriate services in connection with pregnancy, confinement, and the post-natal period," with free services when necessary. They are also entitled to adequate nutrition during pregnancy and lactation.

In education, women are recognized as having the right to the same conditions as men for career and vocational guidance, for access to academic and other studies, and for the achievement of diplomas in educational institutions in and of all categories, in rural as well as urban areas. Women should also enjoy the right of access to the same curricula and examinations, teaching staff with qualifications of the same standard, and school premises as well as equipment of the same quality. Human rights instruments call for the elimination of stereotyped concepts of the role of men and women at all levels and in all forms of education through the encouragement of coeducation, through the same benefits from scholarships and study grants, through the same access to continuing education, and through the same chances to participate actively in sports and physical education. States are also pledged to reduce the female student dropout rates and organize programs for girls and women who have left school prematurely.

In the areas of marriage and family, Article 16 of CEDAW confers on women, on the basis of equality with men, the same rights to enter into marriage only with their free and full consent, to decide freely on the number and spacing of their children, and to have access to information, education, and other means to enable them to exercise these rights. Further, women share with men the same rights and responsibilities as parents, regardless of marital status, in matters relating to children as well as guardianship, wardship, trusteeship and adoption of children, or similar institutions where these concepts exist in legislation. Wives and husbands have the same personal rights, including the right to choose a family name, a profession, and an occupation; both spouses have the same right with respect to the ownership, acquisition, management, administration, enjoyment and disposition of property.

Any discussion of women's rights should perhaps be accompanied by some evaluation of the issues of employment, education, health and marital relations. So we will generally look at each, although we can but touch the surface.

The focus on employment in the human rights instruments under emphasis should not be regarded as simply ensuring that women have jobs, important as this is and has been. Employment should be seen in a more fundamental light: women, as in the case of all human beings, have an equal right to pursue their material well-being and their spiritual development, in conditions of freedom and dignity as well as economic security—and of course these conditions and developments are significantly dependent on gainful employment.

To the extent that one understands the centrality of employment, one will understand the core importance of education, since without the skills that education helps to develop, equality of opportunity or equal employment prospects are mere abstractions. But education extends to all areas: to one's sense of one's possibilities, to one's perceived competence to make an impact, to one's capacity to participate effectively in public life—from voting and the exercise of functions at the highest levels of government to the shaping of the general environment within which one lives and moves.

With respect to family and the issues of health, we will use but a few illustrations to highlight their far-reaching impact. "Matrimonial regimes" have historically been partial to men in respect of parental rights and obligations. For example, authority frequently belonged exclusively or principally to the father, and in some countries, if that authority were lost, it would not automatically pass to the mother. In many instances, in case of the dissolution of the marriage, custody of the child would be awarded to the father "regardless of the merits of the case."[5] Hence, the relevant human rights instruments support the "same rights and responsibilities of parents" in matters relating to children, guardianship, etc.

The field of health care, although on the surface appearing to concern itself primarily with pregnancy and childbearing, is actually much broader. The above areas are emphasized because they have special significance to the unequal socioeconomic standing of women. One of the particularly controversial areas to which further study is being given is that of operation on women based on custom. Should women, for example, have the right not to undergo "ritual operations" that result in their being genitally mutilated?

There is an area of rights that does not fit into the two general categories previously identified. It relates to the right of women and children during emergencies and in armed conflicts whether such emergencies or conflicts be associated with the struggle for peace, self-determination, national liberation or independence.

Women have the right not to be subjected to, among other things, persecution, degrading treatment and violence, mass arrests, forcible evictions, or destruction of dwellings. Some of these rights are, of course, applicable to the civilian population at large, but special emphasis is given to women and children because they are generally the most vulnerable members of any population.

In concluding this introductory section, we should look briefly at two areas: that of the relationship between the worldwide efforts on the part of women to effect their liberation and the rights we have been discussing, and that of the broader social meaning of those rights in relationship to the evolving international order.

In case of the first, this relationship has been reciprocal and even, at times, mutually reinforcing. While the years immediately following World War II saw the global community, through the United Nations, acting to recognize women as having certain rights, that recognition—in large measure—came as a result of the political pressure that women brought to bear on their respective national governments. These new found rights helped to confer a greater degree of freedom and equality on women who, in turn, pressured their governments even more to take action promotive of gender equality. By the 1960s and the early 1970s, however, women began to discover that these rights were not being publicly discussed, not to mention implemented. In industrial democracies like the United States, few women even knew that international instruments conferred rights for which they were struggling at home—the Equal Rights Amendment, for example. And in Third World countries, most women were often too downtrodden, even if they knew their rights, to do much about their plight. A growing awareness of their common condition (in part informed by certain studies and reports by the United Nations) induced women to embark on a worldwide strategy—one that would seek to marshall the efforts of women throughout the world in a common struggle. That strategy gave support to the United Nations Decade for Women (1976–1985), as well as the 1975 International Women's Year, proclaimed and celebrated by the United Nations.

The period covered by the International Women's Year and the accompanying Decade for Women—a period devoted to intensified action to promote equality between women and men—saw three U.N.-sponsored global conferences on women. These conferences (the 1975 World Conference of the International Women's Year in Mexico City, the 1980 World Conference of the U.N. Decade for Women in Copenhagen, and the 1985 Nairobi World Conference, which reviewed and appraised the U.N. Decade for Women) made important contributions in the international effort to eliminiate discrimination against women.

To the first conference we owe international conscious-raising about the profound nature and complexity of discrimination against women; to the second we owe the program of action that linked the advancement of women to plans for the development and establishment of networks among women on a worldwide scale; and to the last, we owe a forward-looking strategy that envisions that by the year 2000 "all governments should have adequate, comprehensive and coherent *national* policies to abolish all obstacles to the full and equal participation of women in all spheres of society."[6] Those *national* policies, to the extent they are in place, will be about the implementation of the rights we have been discussing.

As regards the broader social meaning of the rights discussed and their relationship to the evolving international order, we can best secure a brief glimpse by employing portions of a U.N. report entitled *The State of the World's Women 1979:*

> Women and girls constitute one-half of the world's population, one-third of its labor force. They perform two-thirds of the world's work hours. They earn, by estimate, only one-tenth of the world's income. They own less than one-hundredth of the world's property. Worldwide, women attend school half as often as men. Two out of every three illiterates are female.[7]

The social meaning of the rights contained in the documents to follow is the liberation of over half the human race. And to bring that half into the full responsibilities of participation, the full joy of independence, and the full light of awareness requires political, socioeconomic and cultural change of a scale never before experienced in human history. Therefore, the women's movement may be properly viewed as constituting a major force for the progressive evolution of the international order and the national societies of which that order is composed.[8]

The volume is divided into seven parts, and within each part, except the last, the included documents are placed in their respective historical order. Each document is preceded by a brief summary of its context and importance. When a part contains several documents, there is a short additional statement that explains their interrelationship. Because a number of conventions from the International Labor Organization are associated with certain important recommendations, some of these recommendations are included and will follow the convention they are designed to complement.

An appendix is incorporated to achieve, among others, two purposes: To expose the reader to the content of two inter–American conventions which bear on women's rights, although they do not have the global focus of the volume; and to identify a number of international conventions which, though largely superseded by the instruments whose contents are included in the volume, bear some historical importance.

Notes on Terminology

Accession or Adhesion: These are two terms that are used interchangeably and describe the formal act or practice by
which a state which has not signed or ratified a treaty,
assumes the obligation of that treaty. No state has an
automatic right to accede to a treaty; usually the possibility as well as the method of accession is contained in
the treaty itself. See, for example, Article 5 of the Convention on the Nationality of Married Women.

Adoption: The formal act by which states that have negotiated a
treaty accept the text of that treaty, as distinct from the
obligations of its terms, as representing what they have
negotiated. The progress of adoption varies; but if a treaty
were negotiated at an international conference, for example, its text may be adopted by a two-thirds vote or by any
other percentage as might have been agreed upon.

Convention: A name given to certain written agreements concluded between states. A more general term is treaty, but
other expressions such as covenant, protocol, compact,
accord, charter, or declaration are, from time to time,
used also.

Declaration: A formal statement of agreement between or among
states. Because declarations do not generally require
ratification and to that extent do not correspond to
treaties in an orthodox sense, many have argued that they
should not have obligatory force. Such is not always the
case, however, and one has but to look to the Universal
Declaration of Human Rights. See Convention above.

Entry into Force: An expression which means the date on which
a treaty or other international agreement begins to have
legal application or to take legal effect. Usually a treaty
enters into force in a manner and at a date provided by

its terms, and it takes effect on those who have accepted
(through ratification or otherwise) its obligations.

Party: A person or group (the state in this volume) participating,
or which has participated, in an international agreement
or other transaction.

Ratification: An act by which modern international treaties
become binding on the parties to it. Although a treaty is
said to be concluded as soon as mutual agreement is
arrived at and indicated by the signature of the parties
which negotiated it, its binding or obligatory force is often
deferred until ratification takes place. Each state has its
own ratification process. (It may also be observed that
"acceptance" or "approval" are terms sometimes used to
indicate a state's consent to be bound by a treaty.)

Recommendation: This term refers to one or two forms by which
the International Labor Organization lays down international standards to improve the conditions of life and
work. One form is through conventions with their usual
legal obligations; the other is through recommendations
which are not ratifiable and impose no legal obligation.
However, because they represent international consensus
and aim to serve as guidelines for national policy in
specific fields where there are legal obligations, they have
important moral force. Other international organizations
or their organs can also make recommendations, the
General Assembly of the UN, for example.

Resolution: As used in this work, it is an international term for the
formal expression of a consensus by an intergovern-
mental body (one whose members are states). Like declarations, resolutions do not require ratification, and create
binding international legal obligations only when they are
accepted in practice by the state adopting them.

Signatory: A state or other inter-governmental entity that has signed an international agreement.

Signature: The act by which a state, through its duly authorized agent, signs its name. Usually, the signing of an agreement previously negotiated indicates provisional acceptance, with final acceptance normally coming at ratification. On rare occasions international agreements can become binding through signature only.

State/Nation: The term state is used interchangeably with nation-state and nation to mean political collectivities that enjoy sovereign independence.

List of Abbreviations

The following abbreviations are used in this volume:

A.	General Assembly
Add.	Addendum
Bevans	U.S. Treaties and Other International Agreements of the United States 1776–1948 (Compiled by C.E. Bevans)
CEDAW	Convention on the Elimination of All Forms of Discrimination Against Women
CONF.	Conference
CSW	U.N. Commission on the Status of Women
ECOSOC or E.	Economic & Social Council
ICRC	International Committee of the Red Cross
ILO	International Labor Organization
L.N.T.S.	League of Nations Treaty Series
Res.	Resolution
Rev.	Revision
Stat.	Statute (U.S.)
Supp.	Supplement
T.I.A.S.	U.S. Treaties and Other International Acts Series

T.S.	U.S. Treaty Series
UNESCO	United Nations Educational, Scientific and Cultural Organizations
UDHR	Universal Declaration of Human Rights
U.N. Doc.	United Nations Document
UNGAOR	United Nations General Assembly Official Records
U.N.T.S.	United Nations Treaty Series
U.S.T.	U.S. Treaties and Other International Agreements

I. The U.N. Charter and the International Bill of Rights

At the legal, moral and political cornerstone of women's rights in international relations are the Charter of the United Nations and the International Bill of Rights. The Bill (composed of the Universal Declaration of Human Rights, The International Covenant on Civil and Political Rights and the International Covenant on Economic, Social and Cultural Rights) is generally acknowledged to be a historical milestone in the struggle for human freedom and dignity. Its conception, creation and development have primarily been the result of actions taken by the United Nations which is required by its charter to take certain steps to promote the rights of individuals, including women.

While the United Nations, as will be later seen, is not the first inter-governmental body to deal with questions relating to the status of women, its charter, which is the most important and widely ratified international agreement making reference to women, is the first international instrument to mention equal rights of women and men in specific terms. It is therefore appropriate to begin an international documentary source of women's rights with a focus on the portions of the charter that are directly related to those rights. Those portions can be said to observe five principles: one of affirmation, one of purpose, one of limitation on what the United Nations itself may not do, another of pledged cooperation, and still another on the objectives of the Trusteeship Council.

The Universal Declaration of Human Rights (UDHR) was proclaimed by the General Assembly on December 10, 1948, and is today regarded as a "common standard of achievement for all peoples and all nations."[1] It calls on every individual and every organ of society to "strive by teaching and education to promote respect for these rights and freedoms and by progressive measures, national and international, to secure their *universal and effective* recognition and observance" (emphasis added).[2] Its great moral authority notwithstanding, the UDHR was never intended to provide the type of specific and comprehensive details of the recognized rights deemed necessary to protect the interests and needs of human beings. So nation-states agreed to adopt other instruments that would refine and make more specific the general principles as well as moral and legal entitlements found in the declaration.

The results are, among others, the two companion instruments to the UDHR—the International Covenant on Civil and Political Rights and the International Covenant on Economic, Social and Cultural Rights. And if the UDHR has been seen as a formal and solemn instrument having a place "suitable for rare occasions when principles of great and lasting importance are being enuciated,"[3] the covenants are no less so. Indeed, the very choice of the word "covenant" (instead of terms such as convention or declaration) to label those two agreements was designed to emphasize their solemn character. Bringing the two covenants into being was no easy task, however. It took some eighteen years after the UDHR to have them adopted (1966); and only after another ten years did they come into effect.

States, divided along ideological lines, sought to give emphasis to certain preferred values. Western countries, for example, sought to give greater weight to civil and political rights; and it was as a result of those countries' insistence that the rights discussed were placed in two separate documents. On the other hand, socialist states and a number of Third World countries had clear preference for economic, social and cultural rights. Today, although the latter class of rights are rarely included in public discussions of human rights in the United

States, they are, as stated by one scholar, "not merely exhortation and aspiration"; they "are as 'human,' universal and fundamental" as are those of the civil and political category.[4]

There is an important legal link between the U.N. Charter and the International Bill of Rights. In Article 56 of the U.N. Charter, nation-states pledge "to take joint and separate action," in cooperation with the United Nations, to achieve universal respect for human rights without distinction as to race, sex, language or religion. That pledge was, by and large, a major impetus in the effort to adopt the UDHR.

There are some issues which should be pointed out regarding the International Bill of Rights and its relationship to the rights of women: the attitude of some governments toward those rights, the referential *nature* of the UDHR, the progressive specificity in the content of rights recognized, and in the early distinction drawn between person and status.

In case of the attitudes of governments, there were those that were clearly opposed to the then emerging international emphasis on gender as a recognized legal and moral category. South Africa, for example—and that state was one of the leaders in advancing the idea of human rights—found unacceptable the proposed Article 1 of the UDHR, which stated that "all human beings are born free and equal in fundamental rights and freedoms." Reason? Equality of rights was unthinkable; "men and women had and always would have different rights," it argued.[5]

Earlier in this background statement, we referred to the moral and legal authority of the UDHR. This moral and legal standing will become particularly obvious in the instruments dealing with women's rights, as they again and again point to it (as well as the U.N. Charter) as a referent. For historical and other perspectives, one will be well-served by also noting the progression in the specific character of the rights relating to women. In the U.N. Charter, one finds reference to "the equal rights of men and women and of nations large and small." In the UDHR we have the type of generalization found in the U.N. Charter but also the more particular claim that "motherhood and childhood are entitled to special assistance." By the time we come to the International Covenant on Economic, Social and Cultural Rights we have recognition of the right to "fair wages and equal remuneration" for work of equal value without distinction as to sex. And this leads us to the matter of a distinction between person and status.

In the immediately preceding paragraph, we made reference to motherhood. Motherhood, as distinct from the individual who occupies the status, is said to enjoy privileges, not rights. Only a person can have rights.[6]

It should be observed that the international covenants recognize rights well beyond those found in the more democratic countries. So, in addition to rights for the criminally accused and rights to free speech and press, one finds the right to self-determination, to nationality at birth, to leave and return to one's country, to form trade unions, to equal remuneration for equal work, to education, to the highest attainable standard of physical and mental health, and to an adequate standard of living. The implementation of the covenants, especially that on economic, social and cultural rights, envision a very important role for the International Labor Organization (ILO).

The expectation of such a role for the ILO was appropriate. Although the covenants are fairly specific about many of the rights recognized, there were many gaps left unfilled by the drafters. For example, Article 10 of the International Covenant on Economic, Social and Cultural Rights recognizes the right of mothers to "special protection" for a "reasonable period before and after childbirth," but gives no indication of what that protection should be or what "reasonable period" means. The ILO Convention Concerning Maternity Protection defines that special protection and specifies the duration of "reasonable period." Hence, part of the role of the ILO has been to give very specific content to some of the more general rights and principles contained in the covenants.

The following documents are not presented in their entirety. The sections of the documents having no relevance to the rights of women were omitted.

The Charter of the United Nations
[Relevant Passages Only]

Preamble

WE THE PEOPLES OF THE UNITED NATIONS DETERMINED

To reaffirm faith in fundamental human rights, in the dignity and worth of the human person, in the equal rights of men and women and of all nations large and small....

Article 1 (3)

To achieve international cooperation in solving international problems of an economic, social, cultural, or humanitarian character, and in promoting and encouraging respect for human rights and fundamental freedoms for all without distinction as to race, sex, language or religion....

Article 8

The United Nations shall place no restrictions on the eligibility of men and women to participate in any capacity and under conditions of equality in its principal and subsidiary organs.

Article 13 (1) (b)

The General Assembly shall initiate studies and make recommendations for the purpose of:

promoting international cooperation in economic, social, cultural, educational, and health fields, and assisting in the realization of human rights and fundamental freedoms for all without distinction as to race, sex, language, or religion.

Article 55 (c)

With a view to the creation of conditions of stability and well-being which are necessary for peaceful and friendly relations among nations based on respect for the principle of equal rights and self-destruction of peoples, the United Nations shall promote:

universal respect for, and observance of, human rights and fundamental freedoms for all without distinction as to race, sex, language or religion.

Article 56

All members pledge themselves to joint and separate action in cooperation with the Organization for the achievement of the purposes set forth in Article 55.

Article 76 (c)

The basic objective of the trusteeship system, in accordance with the Purposes of the United Nations laid down in Article 1 of the present Charter, shall be:

> to encourage respect for human rights and for fundamental freedoms for all without distinction as to race, sex, language, or religion, and to encourage recognition of the interdependence of the peoples of the world. . . .

The Universal Declaration of Human Rights

[Relevant Passages Only]

Article 2 (1)

Everyone is entitled to all rights and freedoms set forth in this Declaration, without distinction of any kind, such as race, colour, sex, language, religion, political or other opinion, national or social origin, property, birth or other status.

Article 16

1. Men and women of full age, without limitation due to race, nationality or religion, have the right to marry and to found a family. They are entitled to equal rights as to marriage, during marriage and at its dissolution.

2. Marriage shall be entered into only with the free and full consent of the intending spouse.

3. The family is the natural and fundamental group unit of society and is entitled to protection by society and the State.

Article 25

1. Everyone has the right to a standard of living adequate for the health and well-being of himself and his family, including food, clothing, housing and medical care and necessary medical services, and the right to security in the event of unemployment, sickness, disability, widowhood, old age or other lack of livelihood in circumstances beyond his control.

2. Motherhood and childhood are entitled to special care and assistance. All children, whether born in or out of wedlock, shall enjoy special protection.

Article 26 (3)

Parents have a prior right to choose the kind of education that shall be given to their children.

The International Covenant on Civil and Political Rights

[Relevant Passages Only]

Article 2 (1)

Each State Party to the present Covenant undertakes to respect and to ensure to all individuals within its territory and subject to its jurisdiction the rights recognized in the present Covenant, without distinction of any kind, such as race, colour, sex, language, religion, political or other opinion, national or social origin, birth or other status.

Article 3

The State Parties to the present Covenant undertake to respect and to ensure the equal right of men and women to the enjoyment of all civil and political rights set forth in the present Covenant.

Article 4 (1)

In time of public emergency which threatens the life of the nation and the existence of which is officially proclaimed, the States Parties to the present Covenant may take measures derogating from their obligations under the present Covenant to the extent strictly required by the exigencies of the situation, provided that such measures are not inconsistent with their other obligations under international law and do not involve discrimination solely on the ground of race, colour, sex, language, religion or social origin.

Article 23

1. The family is the natural and fundamental group unit of society and is entitled to protection by society and the State.

2. The right of men and women of marriageable age to marry and to found a family shall be recognized.

3. No marriage shall be entered into without the free and full consent of the intending spouses.

4. State Parties to the present Covenant shall take appropriate steps to ensure equality of rights and responsibilities of spouses as to marriage, during marriage and at its dissolution. In case of dissolution, provisions shall be made for the necessary protection of any children.

Article 24 (1)

Every child shall have, without discrimination as to race, colour, sex, language, religion, national or social origin, property or birth, the right to such measures of protection as are required by his status as a minor, on the part of the family, society and the State.

Article 25

Every citizen shall have the right and the opportunity, without any of the distinctions mentioned in Article 2 and without unreasonable restrictions:

a. to take part in the conduct of public affairs, directly or through freely chosen representatives;

b. vote and be elected at genuine periodic elections which shall be by universal and equal suffrage and shall be held by secret ballot, guaranteeing the free expression of the will of the electors;

c. to have access, on general terms of equality, to public service in his country.

The International Covenant on Economic, Social and Cultural Rights

[Relevant Passages Only]

Article 2 (2)

The States Parties to the present Covenant undertake to guarantee that the rights enunciated in the present Covenant will be exercised without discrimination of any kind as to race, colour, sex, language, religion, political or other opinion, national or social origin, property, birth or other status.

Article 3

The States Parties to the present Covenant undertake to ensure the equal right of men and women to the enjoyment of all economic, social and cultural rights set forth in the present Covenant.

Article 7 (a) (i, ii) (c)

The States Parties to the present Covenant recognize the right of everyone to the enjoyment of just and favorable conditions of work which ensure, in particular:

(a) Remuneration which provide workers, as a minimum, with:

   (i) fair wages and equal remuneration for work of equal value without distinction of any kind, in particular women being guaranteed conditions of work not inferior to those enjoyed by men, with equal pay for equal work;

   (ii) a decent living for themselves and their families in accordance with the provisions of the present Covenant;

(c) Equal opportunity for everyone to be promoted in his employment to an appropriate higher level, subject to no considerations other than those of seniority and competence.

Article 10 (1) (2)

The States Parties to the present Covenant recognize that:

1. The widest possible protection and assistance should be accorded to the family, which is the natural and fundamental group unit of society, particularly for its establishment and while it is responsible for the care and education of dependent children. Marriage must be entered into with the free consent of the intending spouses.

2. Special protection should be accorded mothers during a reasonable period before and after childbirth. During such period working mothers should be accorded paid leave or leave with adequate social security benefits.

II.   Employment, Remuneration and Education

This section of the work presents documents from two specialized agencies of the United Nations—the International Labor Organization (ILO) and the United Nations Educational, Scientific and Cultural Organization (UNESCO).

The ILO, located in Geneva, Switzerland, was originally established in 1919 under the League of Nations. The ILO is made up of an all-member International Labor Conference, a governing body and a secretariat called the International Labor Office. Its function is the improvement of working conditions in member nations by the establishment of labor standards and the mobilization of world opinion to support those standards. Among its specific areas of focus are health, social security, and full employment. It is asserted in the ILO's constitution that protection of women's interests is part of its pursuit of social justice.[1]

The primary function of UNESCO, which has its headquarters in Paris, France, has been to promote cooperation among member states in the fields of education, science and culture. Through recommendations to its members and through its own activities, UNESCO has carried out exchange programs, promoted teaching and research, and has sought to advance the ideals of equal rights and educational opportunities for all "without regard ... to sex and any other distinction."[2]

Convention (No. 40) Concerning Compulsory Widows' and Orphans' Insurance for Persons Employed in Agricultural Undertakings

[Vol. 39 U.N.T.S., p. 285]

Editor's Comments. *Among the earlier international legal instruments adopted by the ILO is the Convention Concerning Compulsory Widows' and Orphans' Insurance for Persons Employed in Agricultural Undertakings. Adopted on June 29, 1933, the convention is really a survivor's insurance treaty for the protection of widows and orphans. In fact, in its preamble, it specifically states that the treaty "may be cited as the Survivors' Insurance (Agriculture) Convention."*

Now, as at the time of its adoption, the convention is rather important because, among other reasons, there is a pattern of behavior among governments to give greater emphasis to the concerns of urban and industrial workers who are usually greater in number and tend to be more politically conscious. The plan incorporated in the treaty applies to all manual and non-manual workers, including apprentices, employed in "agricultural undertakings." It also applies to domestic servants employed by households of agricultural employers. Member states which ratify the convention undertake to set up (or if they already have one, to maintain it) a scheme of insurance that will, at a minimum, *be the equivalent of that recommended by the treaty. And what is the minimum? Article 6 is fairly explicit in stating it: the widows' and orphans' insurance scheme "shall at a minimum confer pension rights on widows who have not remarried and children of a deceased insured or pensioned person." There are, of course, circumstances under which exceptions are allowed. For example, if the person is already receiving another pension that adequately protects the widow.*

The convention came into force September 29, 1949. The full text follows.

The General Conference of the International Labour Organisation,

Having been convened at Geneva by the Governing Body
of the International Labour Office, and having met in its
Seventeenth Session on 8 June 1933, and

Having decided upon the adoption of certain proposals with
regard to compulsory widows' and orphans' insurance,
which is included in the second item on the agenda of the
Session, and

Having determined that these proposals shall take the form
of an international Convention,

adopts this twenty-ninth day of June of the year one thousand
nine hundred and thirty-three the following Convention, which
may be cited as the Survivors' Insurance (Agriculture) Convention, 1933, for ratification by the Members of the International
Labour Organisation, in accordance with the provisions of the
Constitution of the International Labour Organisation:

Article 1

Each Member of the International Labour Organisation
which ratifies this Convention undertakes to set up or maintain
a scheme of compulsory widows' and orphans' insurance which
shall be based on provisions at least equivalent to those contained in this convention.

Article 2

1. The compulsory widows' and orphans' insurance scheme
shall apply to manual and non-manual workers, including
apprentices, employed in agricultural undertakings, and to
domestic servants employed in the households of agricultural
employers.

2. Provided that any Member may in its national laws or
regulations make such exceptions as it deems necessary in
respect of—

(a) workers whose remuneration exceeds a prescribed amount
and, where national laws or regulations do not make this
exception general in its application, any non-manual
workers engaged in occupations which are ordinarily considered as liberal professions;

(b) workers who are not paid a money wage;

(c) young workers under a prescribed age and workers too old to become insured when they first enter employment;

(d) outworkers whose conditions of work are not of a like nature to those of ordinary wage earners;

(e) members of the employer's family;

(f) workers whose employment is of such a nature that, its total duration being necessarily short, they cannot qualify for benefit, and persons engaged solely in occasional or subsidiary employment;

(g) invalid workers and workers in receipt of an invalidity or old-age pension;

(h) retired public officials employed for remuneration and persons possessing a private income, where the retirement pension or private income is at least equal to the invalidity pension provided by national laws or regulations;

(i) workers who, during their studies, give lessons or work for remuneration in preparation for an occupation corresponding to such studies.

3. Provided also that there may be exempted from liability to insurance persons whose survivors will, by virtue of any law, regulations or special scheme, become entitled to benefits at least equivalent on the whole to those provided for in this Convention.

Article 3

National laws or regulations shall, under conditions to be determined by them, either entitle persons formerly compulsorily insured who are not in receipt of a pension to continue their insurance voluntarily or entitle such persons to maintain their rights by the periodical payment of a fee for the purpose, unless the said rights are automatically maintained or, in the case of married women, the husband, if not liable to compulsory insurance, is permitted to insure voluntarily and thereby to qualify his wife for an old-age or widow's pension.

Article 4

1. Notwithstanding the provisions of Article 5, the right to a pension may be made conditional upon the completion of a qualifying period, which may involve the payment of a minimum number of contributions since entry into insurance and during a prescribed period immediately preceding the happening of the event insured against.

2. The duration of the qualifying period shall not exceed 60 contribution months, 250 contribution weeks or 1,500 contribution days.

3. Where the completion of the qualifying period involves the payment of a prescribed number of contributions during a prescribed period immediately preceding the happening of the event assured against, periods for which benefit has been paid in respect of temporary incapacity for work or of unemployment shall be reckoned as contribution periods to such extent and under such conditions as may be determined by national laws or regulations.

Article 5

1. An insured person who ceases to be liable to insurance without being entitled to a benefit representing a return for the contributions credited to his account shall retain his rights in respect of these contributions.

2. Provided that national laws or regulations may terminate rights in respect of contributions on the expiry of a term which shall be reckoned from the date when the insured person so ceased to be liable to insurance and which shall be either variable or fixed.

(a) Where the term is variable, it shall not be less than one-third (less the periods for which contributions have not been credited) of the total of the periods for which contributions have been credited since entry into insurance.

(b) Where the term is fixed, it shall in no case be less than eighteen months and rights in respect of contributions may

be terminated on the expiry of the term unless, in the course thereof, a minimum number of contributions prescribed by national laws or regulations have been credited to the account of the insured person in virtue of either compulsory or voluntarily continued insurance.

Article 6

The widows' and orphans' insurance scheme shall as a minimum confer pension rights on widows who have not remarried and the children of a deceased insured or pensioned person.

Article 7

1. The right to a widow's pension may be reserved to widows who are above a prescribed age or are invalid.

2. The provisions of paragraph 1 shall not apply in the case of special schemes for non-manual workers.

3. The right to a widow's pension may be restricted to cases where the marriage has lasted for a prescribed period and was contracted before the insured or pensioned person had reached a prescribed age or become invalid.

4. The right to a widow's pension may be withheld if, at the time of the death of the insured or pensioned person, the marriage had been dissolved or if a separation had been pronounced in proceedings in which the wife was found solely at fault.

5. Where there are several claimants to a widow's pension, the amount payable may be limited to that of one pension.

Article 8

1. Any child who has not reached a prescribed age which shall not be less than fourteen shall be entitled to a pension in respect of the death of either parent.

2. Provided that the right to a pension in respect of the death of an insured or pensioned mother may either be made

conditional upon the mother's having contributed to the support of the child or be made conditional upon her having been a widow at the time of her death.

3. National laws or regulations shall determine the cases in which a child other than a legitimate child shall be entitled to a pension.

Article 9

1. The pension shall, whether or not dependent of the time spent in insurance, be a fixed sum or a percentage of the remuneration taken into account for insurance purposes or vary with the amount of the contributions paid.

2. Where the pension varies with the time spent in insurance and its award is made conditional upon the completion by the insured person of a qualifying period, the pension shall, unless a minimum rate is guaranteed, include a fixed sum or fixed portion not dependent on the time spent in insurance; where the pension is awarded without any condition as to the completion of a qualifying period, provision may be made for a guaranteed minimum rate of pension.

3. Where contributions are graduated according to remuneration, the remuneration taken into account for this purpose shall also be taken into account for the purpose of computing the pension, whether or not the pension varies with the time spent in insurance.

Article 10

Insurance institutions shall be authorised, under conditions which shall be determined by national laws or regulations, to grant benefits in kind for the purpose of preventing, postponing, alleviating or curing invalidity to persons who are in receipt of or may be entitled to claim a pension on the ground of invalidity.

Article 11

1. The right to benefits may be forfeited or suspended in whole or in part—

(*a*) if death has been caused by a criminal offence committed or the wilful misconduct of the insured person or any person who may become entitled to a survivor's pension; or

(*b*) if the insured person or any person who may become entitled to a survivor's pension has acted fraudulently towards the insurance institution.

2. The pension may be suspended in whole or in part while the person concerned—

(*a*) is entirely maintained at the public expense or by a social insurance institution;

(*b*) refuses without valid reason to comply with the doctor's orders or the instructions relating to the conduct of invalids or voluntarily and without authorisation removes herself from the supervision of the insurance institution;

(*c*) is in receipt of another periodical cash benefit payable by virtue of any law or regulations concerning compulsory social insurance, pensions or workmen's compensation for accidents or occupational diseases;

(*d*) having been awarded a widow's pension without any condition as to age or invalidity, is living with a man as his wife; or

(*e*) in the case of special schemes for non-manual workers, is in receipt of remuneration exceeding a prescribed rate.

Article 12

1. The insured persons and their employers shall contribute to the financial resources of the insurance scheme.

2. National laws or regulations may exempt from liability to pay contributions—

(*a*) apprentices and young workers under a prescribed age;

(*b*) workers who are not paid a money wage or whose wages are very low;

(*c*) workers in the service of an employer who pays contributions assessed on a basis which is not dependent on the number of workers employed.

3. Contributions from employers may be dispensed with under laws or regulations concerning schemes of national insurance not restricted in scope to employed person.

4. The public authorities shall contribute to the financial resources or to the benefits of insurance schemes covering employed persons in general or manual workers.

5. National laws or regulations which, at the time of the adoption of this Convention, do not require contributions from insured persons may continue not to require such contributions.

Article 13

1. The insurance scheme shall be administered by institutions founded by the public authorities and not conducted with a view to profit, or by State insurance funds.

2. Provided that national laws or regulations may also entrust its administration to institutions founded on the initiative of the parties concerned or of their organisations and duly approved by the public authorities.

3. The funds of insurance institutions and State insurance funds shall be administered separately from the public funds.

4. Representatives of the insured persons shall participate in the management of insurance institutions under conditions to be determined by national laws or regulations, which may likewise decide as to the participation of representatives of employers and of the public authorities.

5. Self-governing insurance institutions shall be under the administrative and financial supervision of the public authorities.

Article 14

1. The survivors of a deceased insured or pensioned person shall have a right of appeal in any dispute concerning benefits.

2. Such disputes shall be referred to special tribunals which shall include judges, whether professional or not, who are specially cognisant of the purposes of insurance or are

assisted by assessors chosen as representative of insured persons and employers respectively.

3. In any dispute concerning liability to insurance or the rate of contribution, the employed person and, in the case of schemes providing for an employer's contribution, his employer shall have a right of appeal.

Article 15

1. Foreign employed persons shall be liable to insurance and to the payment of contributions under the same conditions as nationals.

2. The survivors of foreign insured or pensioned persons shall be entitled under the same conditions as nationals to the benefits derived from the contributions credited to their account.

3. The survivors of foreign insured or pensioned persons shall, if nationals of a Member which is bound by this Convention and the laws or regulations of which therefore provide for a State subsidy towards the financial resources or benefits of the insurance scheme in conformity with Article 12, also be entitled to any subsidy or supplement to or fraction of a pension which is payable out of public funds.

4. Provided that national laws or regulations may restrict to nationals the right to any subsidy or supplement to or fraction of a pension which is payable out of public funds and granted solely to the survivors of insured persons who have exceeded a prescribed age at the date when the laws or regulations providing for compulsory insurance come into force.

5. Any restrictions which may apply in the event of residence abroad shall only apply to pensioners who are nationals of any Member bound by this Convention and reside in the territory of any Member bound thereby to the extent to which they apply to nationals of the country in which the pension has been acquired. Provided that any subsidy or supplement to or fraction of a pension which is payable out of public funds may be withheld.

Article 16

1. The insurance of employed persons shall be governed by the law applicable at their place of employment.

2. In the interest of continuity of insurance exceptions may be made to this rule by agreement between the Members concerned.

Article 17

Any member may prescibe special provisions for frontier workers whose place of employment is in its territory and whose place of residence is abroad.

Article 18

In countries which, at the time when this Convention first comes into force, have no laws or regulations providing for compulsory widows' and orphans' insurance, an existing non-contributory pension scheme which guarantees an individual right to a pension under the conditions defined in Articles 19 to 25 hereinafter shall be deemed to satisfy the requirements of this Convention.

Article 19

1. The following shall be entitled to a pension:

(a) every widow who has not remarried and who has at least two dependent children;

(b) every orphan, that is to say, every child who has lost both parents.

2. National laws or regulations shall define—

(a) the cases in which a child other than a legitimate child shall be deemed to be the child of a widow for the purpose of entitling her to a pension;

(b) the age until which a child shall be considered dependent upon a widow or shall be entitled to an orphan's pension: Provided that this age shall in no case be less than fourteen.

Article 20

1. The right to a widow's pension may be made conditional upon the residence in the territory of the Member—

(*a*) of the deceased husband during a period immediately preceding his death; and

(*b*) of the widow during a period immediately preceding the making of her claim for a pension.

2. The right to an orphan's pension may be made conditional upon the residence, in the territory of the Member during a period immediately preceding death, of whichever of the parents died the more recently.

3. The period of residence in the territory of the Member to have been completed by a widow or deceased parent shall be prescribed by national laws or regulations but shall not exceed five years.

Article 21

1. A claimant shall be entitled to a widow's or orphan's pension if the annual value of the claimant's means, including any means of dependent children or orphans, does not exceed a limit which shall be fixed by national laws or regulations with due regard to the minimum cost of living.

2. Means up to a level which shall be determined by national laws or regulations shall be exempted for the purpose of the assessment of means.

Article 22

The rate of pension shall be an amount which, together with any means of the claimant in excess of the means exempted, is at least sufficient to cover the essential needs of the pensioner.

Article 23

1. A claimant shall have a right of appeal in any dispute concerning the award of a pension or the rate thereof.

2. The appeal shall lie to an authority other than the authority which gave the decision in the first instance.

Article 24

1. Foreign widows and orphans shall, if nationals of a Member bound by this Convention, be entitled to pensions under the same conditions as nationals.

2. Provided that national laws or regulations may make the award of a pension to foreigners conditional upon the completion of a period of residence in the territory of the Member which shall not exceed by more than five years the period of residence provided for in Article 20.

Article 25

1. The right to a pension may be forfeited or suspended in whole or in part if the widow or the person who has undertaken responsibility for the care of the orphan has obtained or attempted to obtain a pension by fraud.

2. The pension may be suspended in whole or in part while the person concerned is entirely maintained at the public expense.

Article 26

Subject to the provisions of paragraph 5 of Article 15, this Convention does not refer to the maintenance of pension rights in the event of residence abroad.

Article 27

The formal ratifications of this Convention under the conditions set forth in the Constitution of the International Labour Organisation shall be communicated to the Director-General of the International Labour Office for registration.

Article 28

1. This Convention shall be binding only upon those

Members whose ratifications have been registered with the International Labour Office.

2. It shall come into force twelve months after the date on which the ratifications of two Members of the International Labour Organisation have been registered with the Director-General.

3. Thereafter, this Convention shall come into force for any Member twelve months after the date on which its ratification has been registered.

Article 29

As soon as the ratifications of two Members of the International Labour Organisation have been registered with the International Labour Office, the Director-General of the International Labour Office shall so notify all the Members of the International Labour Organisation. He shall likewise notify them of the registration of ratifications which may be communicated subsequently by other Members of the Organisation.

Article 30

1. A Member which has ratified this Convention may denounce it after the expiration of ten years from the date on which the Convention first comes into force, by an act communicated to the Director-General of the International Labour Office for registration. Such denunciation shall not take effect until one year after the date on which it is registered with the International Labour Office.

2. Each Member which has ratified this Convention and which does not, within the year following the expiration of the period of ten years mentioned in the preceding paragraph, exercise the right of denunciation provided for in this Article, will be bound for another period of ten years and, thereafter, may denounce this Convention at the expiration of each period of ten years under the terms provided for in this Article.

Article 31

At the expiration of each period of ten years after the coming into force of this Convention, the Governing Body of the International Labour Office shall present to the General Conference a report on the working of this Convention and shall consider the desirability of placing on the agenda of the Conference the question of its revision in whole or in part.

Article 32

1. Should the Conference adopt a new Convention revising this Convention in whole or in part, then, unless the new Convention otherwise provides,

(a) the ratification by Member of the new revising Convention shall *ipso jure* involve the immediate denunciation of this Convention, notwithstanding the provisions of Article 30 above, if and when the new revising Convention shall have come into force;

(b) as from the date when the new revising Convention comes into force, this Convention shall cease to be open to ratification by the Members.

2. This Convention shall in any case remain in force in its actual form and content for those Members which have ratified it but have not ratified the revising Convention.

Article 33

The French and English texts of this Convention shall both be authentic.

The foregoing is the authentic text of the Survivors' Insurance (Agriculture) Convention, 1933, as modified by the Final Articles Revision Convention, 1946.

Convention (No. 100) Concerning Equal Remuneration for Men and Women Workers for Work of Equal Value

[Vol. 165 U.N.T.S., p. 303]

Editor's Comments. *One of the areas of social life that invites some of the most vexing questions is that concerning the inequality in compensation that women and men receive for equivalent work. As previously indicated in the introduction, the United Nations has sought to remove that inequality. But the institution most directly responsible for specific proposals to that end has been the ILO.*

On June 29, 1951, the General Conference of the ILO adopted what is today called the Equal Remuneration Convention[3] which requires that states "ensure the application to all workers of the principle of equal remuneration for men and women workers for work of equal value." The term "remuneration," as used in the treaty, includes the "ordinary, basic or minimum wage or salary and any additional" allowance payable "directly or indirectly, whether in case or in kind, by the employer of the worker."[4] The ILO did more.

On the very day the convention was adopted, the General Conference also accepted a recommendation (No. 90) respecting equal remuneration. That recommendation advised states on what the ILO considers some desirable methods by which the principle of equal compensation for women and men may be effectively carried out, especially as implementation moves from employees of the central government to those of the provincial and local authorities and to all occupations in a given society.

The recommendation is included here not only for its practical suggestions, however. Though not legally binding, it has a certain moral authority that nation-states cannot easily overlook, especially if they seek to advance, as an excuse for non-compliance with their obligation under the convention, the claim of difficulties in implementation. (And here it must be noted that some of the suggestions by the recommendation have been successfully used by certain countries.)

The convention entered into force on May 23, 1953, and has been ratified by over a hundred nation-states. The full text follows.

The General Conference of the International Labour Organisation,

Having been convened at Geneva by the Governing Body of the International Labour Office, and having met in its Thirty-fourth Session on 6 June 1951, and

Having decided upon the adoption of certain proposals with regard to the principle of equal remuneration for men and women workers for work or equal value, which is the seventh item on the agenda of the session, and

Having determined that these proposals shall take the form of an international Convention,

adopts this twenty-ninth day of June of the year one thousand nine hundred and fifty-one the following Convention, which may be cited as the Equal Remuneration Convention, 1951:

Article 1

For the purpose of this Convention—

(a) the term "remuneration" includes the ordinary, basic or minimum wage or salary and any additional emoluments whatsoever payable directly or indirectly, whether in cash or in kind, by the employer to the worker and arising out of the worker's employment;

(b) the term "equal remuneration for men and women workers for work or equal value" refers to rates of remuneration established without discrimination based on sex.

Article 2

1. Each Member shall, by means appropriate to the methods in operation for determining rates of remuneration, promote and, in so far as is consistent with such methods ensure the application to all workers of the principle of equal remuneration for men and women workers for work of equal value.

2. This principle may be applied by means of—

(a) national laws or regulations;

(b) legally established or recognised machinery for wage determination;

(c) collective agreements between employers and workers; or

(d) a combination of these various means.

Article 3

1. Where such action will assist in giving effect to the provisions of this Convention measures shall be taken to promote objective appraisal of jobs on the basis of the work to be performed.

2. The methods to be followed in this appraisal may be decided upon by the authorities responsible for the determination of rates of remuneration, or, where such rates are determined by collective agreements, by the parties thereto.

3. Differential rates between workers which correspond, without regard to sex, to differences, as determined by such objective appraisal, in the work to be performed shall not be considered as being contrary to the principle of equal remuneration for men and women workers for work of equal value.

Article 4

Each Member shall co-operate as appropriate with the employers' and workers' organisations concerned for the purpose of giving effect to the provisions of this Convention.

Article 5

The formal ratifications of this Convention shall be communicated to the Director-General of the International Labour Office for registration.

Article 6

1. This Convention shall be binding only upon those Members of the International Labour Organisation whose ratifications have been registered with the Director-General.

2. It shall come into force twelve months after the date on which the ratifications of two Members have been registered with the Director-General.

3. Thereafter, this Convention shall come into force for any Member twelve months after the date on which its ratification has been registered.

Article 7

1. Declarations communicated to the Director-General of the International Labour Office in accordance with paragraph 2 of Article 35 of the Constitution of the International Labour Organisation shall indicate—

(a) the territories in respect of which the Member concerned undertakes that the provisions of the Convention shall be applied without modification;

(b) the territories in respect of which it undertakes that the provisions of the Convention shall be applied subject to modifications, together with details of the said modifications;

(c) the territories in respect of which the Convention is inapplicable and in such cases the grounds on which it is inapplicable;

(d) the territories in respect of which it reserves its decisions pending further consideration of the position.

2. The undertakings referred to in subparagraphs *(a)* and *(b)* of paragraph 1 of this Article shall be deemed to be an integral part of the ratification and shall have the force of ratification.

3. Any Member may at any time by a subsequent declaration cancel in whole or in part any reservation made in its original declaration in virtue of subparagraph *(b)*, *(c)* or *(d)* of paragraph 1 of this Article.

4. Any Member may, at any time at which the Convention is subject to denunciation in accordance with the provisions of Article 9, communicate to the Director-General a declaration

modifying in any other respect the terms of any former declaration and stating the present position in respect of such territories as it may specify.

Article 8

1. Declarations communicated to the Director-General of the International Labour Office in accordance with paragraph 4 or 5 of Article 35 of the Constitution of the International Labour Organisation shall indicate whether the provisions of the Convention will be applied in the territory concerned without modification or subject to modifications; when the declaration indicates that the provisions of the Convention will be applied subject to modifications, it shall give details of the said modifications.

2. The Member, Members or international authority concerned may at any time by a subsequent declaration renounce in whole or in part the right to have recourse to any modifications indicated in any former declaration.

3. The Member, Members or international authority concerned may, at any time at which this Convention is subject to denunciation in accordance with the provisions of Article 9, communicate to the Director-General a declaration modifying in any other respect the terms of any former declaration and stating the present position in respect of the application of the Convention.

Article 9

1. A Member which has ratified this Convention may denounce it after the expiration of ten years from the date on which the Convention first comes into force, by an act communicated to the Director-General of the International Labour Office for registration. Such denunciation shall not take effect until one year after the date on which it is registered.

2. Each Member which has ratified this Convention and which does not, within the year following the expiration of the period of ten years mentioned in the preceding paragraph,

exercise the right of denunciation provided for in this Article, will be bound for another period of ten years and, thereafter, may denounce this Convention at the expiration of each period of ten years under the terms provided for in this Article.

Article 10

1. The Director-General of the International Labour Office shall notify all Members of the International Labour Organisation of the registration of all ratifications, declarations and denunciations communicated to him by the members of the Organisation.

2. When notifying the Members of the Organisation of the registration of the second ratification communicated to him, the Director-General shall draw the attention of the Members of the Organisation to the date upon which the Convention will come into force.

Article 11

The Director-General of the International Labour Office shall communicate to the Secretary-General of the United Nations for registration in accordance with Article 102 of the Charter of the United Nations full particulars of all ratifications, declarations and acts of denunciation registered by him in accordance with the provisions of the preceding Articles.

Article 12

At such times as it may consider necessary the Governing Body of the International Labour Office shall present to the General Conference a report on the working of this Convention and shall examine the desirability of placing on the agenda of the Conference the question of its revision in whole or in part.

Article 13

1. Should the Conference adopt a new Convention revising this Convention in whole or in part, then unless the new Convention otherwise provides—

(a) the ratification by a Member of the new revising Convention shall *ipso jure* involve the immediate denunciation of this Convention, notwithstanding the provisions of Article 9 above, if and when the new revising Convention shall have come into force;

(b) as from the date when the new revising Convention comes into force this Convention shall cease to be open to ratification by the Members.

2. This Convention shall in any case remain in force in its actual form and content for those Members which have ratified it but have not ratified the revising Convention.

Article 14

The English and French versions of the text of this Convention are equally authoritative.

Recommendation (No. 90) Concerning Equal Remuneration for Men and Women Workers for Work of Equal Value

The General Conference of the International Labour Organisation,

> Having been convened at Geneva by the Governing Body of the International Labour Office, and having met in its Thirty-fourth Session on 6 June 1951, and

> Having decided upon the adoption of certain proposals with regard to the principle of equal remuneration for men and women workers for work of equal value, which is the seventh item on the agenda of the session, and

> Having determined that the proposals shall take the form of a Recommendation supplementing the Equal Remuneration Convention, 1951,

adopts this twenty-ninth day of June of the year one thousand nine hundred and fifty-one the following Recommendation, which may be cited as the Equal Remuneration Recommendation, 1951:

Whereas the Equal Remuneration Convention, 1951, lays down certain general principles concerning equal remuneration for men and women workers for work of equal value;

Whereas the Convention provides that the application of the principle of equal remuneration for men and women workers for work of equal value shall be promoted or ensured by means appropriate to the methods in operation for determining rates of remuneration in the countries concerned;

Whereas it is desirable to indicate certain procedures for the progressive application of the principles laid down in the Convention;

Whereas it is at the same time desirable that all Members should, in applying these principles, have regard to methods of application which have been found satisfactory in certain countries;

The Conference recommends that each Member should, subject to the provisions of Article 2 of the Convention, apply the following provisions and report to the International Labour Office as requested by the Governing Body concerning the measures taken to give effect thereto;

1. Appropriate action should be taken, after consultation with the workers' organisations concerned or, where such organisations do not exist, with the workers concerned—

(a) to ensure the application of the principle of equal remuneration for men and women workers for work or equal value to all employees of central Government departments or agencies; and

(b) to encourage the application of the principle to employees of State, provincial or local Government departments or agencies, where these have jurisdiction over rates of remuneration.

2. Appropriate action should be taken, after consultation with the employers' and workers' organisations concerned to ensure, as rapidly as practicable, the application of the principle of equal remuneration for men and women workers for work of equal value in all occupations, other than those mentioned in Paragraph 1, in which rates or remuneration are subject to statutory regulation or public control, particularly as regards—

(a) the establishment of minimum or other wage rates in industries and services where such rates are determined under public authority;

(b) industries and undertakings operated under public ownership or control; and

(c) where appropriate, work executed under the terms of public contracts.

3. (1) Where appropriate in the light of the methods in operation for the determination of rates of remuneration, provision should be made by legal enactment for the general application of the principle of equal remuneration for men and women workers for work of equal value.

(2) The competent public authority should take necessary and appropriate measures to ensure that employers and workers are fully informed as to such legal requirements and, where appropriate, advised on their application.

4. When, after consultation with the organisations of workers and employers concerned, where such exist, it is not deemed feasible to implement immediately the principle of equal remuneration for men and women workers for work of equal value, in respect of employment covered by Paragraph 1, 2 or 3, appropriate provision should be made or caused to be made, as soon as possible, for its progressive application, by such measures as—

(a) decreasing the differentials between rates of remuneration for men and rates of remuneration for women for work of equal value;

(b) where a system of increments is in force, providing equal increments for men and women workers performing work of equal value.

5. Where appropriate for the purpose of facilitating the determination of rates or remuneration in accordance with the principle of equal remuneration for men and women workers for work or equal value, each Member should, in agreement with the employers' and workers' organisations concerned, establish or encourage the establishment of methods for objective appraisal of the work to be performed, whether by job analysis or by other procedures, with a view to providing a classification of jobs without regard to sex; such methods should be applied in accordance with the provisions of Article 2 of the Convention.

6. In order to facilitate the application of the principle of equal remuneration for men and women workers for work of equal value, appropriate action should be taken, where necessary, to raise the productive efficiency of women workers by such measures as—

(a) ensuring that workers of both sexes have equal or equivalent facilities for vocational guidance or employment counselling, for vocational training and for placement;

(b) taking appropriate measures to encourage women to use facilities for vocational guidance or employment counselling, for vocational training and for placement;

(c) providing welfare and social services which meet the needs of women workers, particularly those with family responsibilities, and financing such services from general public funds or from social security or industrial welfare funds financed by payments made in respect of workers without regard to sex; and

(d) promoting equality of men and women workers as regards access to occupations and posts without prejudice to the provisions of international regulations and of national laws and regulations concerning the protection of the health and welfare of women.

7. Every effort should be made to promote public understanding of the grounds on which it is considered that the principle of equal remuneration for men and women workers for work of equal value should be implemented.

8. Such investigations as may be desirable to promote the application of the principle should be undertaken.

Convention (No. 103) Concerning Maternity Protection (Revised 1952)

[Vol. 214 U.N.T.S., p. 321]

Editor's Comment. *In 1919, the ILO adopted the Convention Concerning the Employment of Women Before and After Childbirth.[5] That treaty sought to establish employment provisions that would give recognition to the special status of women before and after childbirth — a need that had been internationally acknowledged. By 1952, however, it was appropriately realized that the terms of the treaty had to be updated. For example, while the area of employment affected by the 1919 convention was "industrial undertakings," including transportation, the convention did not cover transport by air.[6] There was also the developed awareness that women should be accorded a lengthier maternity leave and greater built-in flexibility to use the time defined by that leave. The result? The adoption by the ILO, on June 29, 1952, of the Convention Concerning Maternity Protection, which is the successor to the above-mentioned 1919 Convention.*

In general, the use of the term "protection" in relationship to women's rights is not encouraged. This is so because such usage can be a distraction in the struggle for gender equality. Within the context of "the maternity circumstances" focused on by the 1952 treaty, however, its use is seen as an acceptable exception.

Under the terms of the convention, the word "woman" means any female person, whether married or not, irrespective of age, nationality, race or creed. And a woman, so defined, when employed in any industrial or commercial undertaking, is entitled to a period of maternity leave of at least twelve weeks. Further, she enjoys the right to a minimum of six weeks compulsory leave after her confinement. And, while on leave, she must receive cash and medical benefits. The amount of money, to be fixed by national law, must be sufficient to ensure "the full and healthy maintenance of herself and her child." Finally, among other things, she may not be dismissed while absent from work during the period of her leave.[7]

By way of comparison or contrast, it might be helpful to look at the relevant section of the European Social Charter, which has sought, in part, to give effect to the obligation of many European states under the Convention Concerning Maternity Protection. States, parties to the Charter, undertake:

    (a)   *to provide either paid leave, by adequate social security benefits or by benefits from public funds for women to take leave before or after childbirth up to a total of at least 12 weeks.*

    (b)   *to consider it unlawful for an employer to give a woman notice of dismissal at such a time that the notice would expire during her absence.*

    (c)   *to provide that mothers who are nursing their infants shall be entitled to sufficient time off for this purpose.*[8]

The Convention Concerning Maternity Protection came into force on September 7, 1955. The full text follows.

The General Conference of the International Labour Organisation,

    Having been convened at Geneva by the Governing Body of the International Labour Office, and having met in its Thirty-fifth Session on 4 June 1952, and

    Having decided upon the adoption of certain proposals with regard to maternity protection, which is the seventh item on the agenda of the session, and

    Having determined that these proposals shall take the form of an international Convention,

adopts this twenty-eighth day of June of the year one thousand nine hundred and fifty-two the following Convention, which may be cited as the Maternity Protection Convention (Revised), 1952.

Article 1

1. This Convention applies to women employed in industrial and agricultural occupations, including women wage earners working at home.

2. For the purpose of this Convention, the term "industrial undertaking" comprises public and private undertaking and any branch thereof and includes particularly—

(a) mines, quarries, and other works for the extraction of minerals from the earth;

(b) undertakings in which articles are manufactured, altered, cleaned, repaired, ornamented, finished, adapted for sale, broken up or demolished, or in which materials are transformed, including undertakings engaged in ship-building, or in the generation, transformation or transmission of electricity or motive power of any kind;

(c) undertakings engaged in building and civil engineering work, including constructional, repair, maintenance, alteration and demolition work;

(d) undertakings engaged in the transport of passengers or goods by road, rail, sea, inland waterway or air, including the handling of goods at docks, quays, wharves, warehouses or airports.

3. For the purpose of this Convention, the term "non-industrial occupations" includes all occupations which are carried on in or in connection with the following undertakings or services, whether public or private:

(a) commercial establishments;

(b) postal and telecommunication services;

(c) establishments and administrative services in which the persons employed are mainly engaged in clerical work;

(d) newspaper undertakings;

(e) hotels, boarding houses, restaurants, clubs, cafés and other refreshment houses;

(f) establishments for the treatment and care of the sick, infirm or destitute and of orphans;

(g) theatres and places of public entertainment;

(h) domestic work for wages in private households;

and any other non-industrial occupations to which the competent authority may decide to apply the provisions of the Convention.

4. For the purpose of this Convention, the term "agricultural occupations" includes all occupations carried on in agricultural undertakings, including plantations and large-scale industrialised agricultural undertakings.

5. In any case in which it is doubtful whether this Convention applies to an undertaking, branch of an undertaking or occupation, the question shall be determined by the competent authority after consultation with the representative organisations of employers and workers concerned where such exist.

6. National laws or regulations may exempt from the application of this Convention undertakings in which only members of the employer's family, as defined by national laws or regulations, are employed.

Article 2

For the purpose of this Convention, the term "woman" means any female person, irrespective of age, nationality, race or creed, whether married or unmarried, and the term "child" means any child whether born of marriage or not.

Article 3

1. A woman to whom this Convention applies shall, on the production of a medical certificate stating the presumed date of her confinement, be entitled to a period of maternity leave.

2. The period of maternity leave shall be at least twelve weeks, and shall include a period of compulsory leave after confinement.

3. The period of compulsory leave after confinement shall be prescribed by national laws or regulations, but shall in no case be less than six weeks; the remainder of the total period of maternity leave may be provided before the presumed date of confinement or following expiration of the compulsory leave period or partly before the presumed date of confinement and partly following the expiration of the compulsory leave period as may be prescribed by national laws or regulations.

4. The leave before the presumed date of confinement shall be extended by any period elapsing between the presumed date of confinement and the actual date of confinement and the period of compulsory leave to be taken after confinement shall not be reduced on that account.

5. In case of illness medically certified arising out of pregnancy, national laws or regulations shall provide for additional leave before confinement, the maximum duration of which may be fixed by the competent authority.

6. In case of illness medically certified arising out of confinement, the woman shall be entitled to an extension of the leave after confinement, the maximum duration of which may be fixed by the competent authority.

Article 4

1. While absent from work on maternity leave in accordance with the provisions of Article 3, the woman shall be entitled to receive cash and medical benefits.

2. The rates of cash benefit shall be fixed by national laws or regulations so as to ensure benefits sufficient for the full and healthy maintenance of herself and her child in accordance with a suitable standard of living.

3. Medical benefits shall include pre-natal, confinement and post-natal care by qualfied midwives or medical practitioners as well as hospitalisation care where necessary; freedom of choice of doctor and freedom of choice between a public and private hospital shall be respected.

4. The cash and medical benefits shall be provided either by means of compulsory social insurance or by means of public funds; in either case they shall be provided as a matter of right to all women who comply with the prescribed conditions.

5. Women who fail to qualify for benefits provided as a matter of right shall be entitled, subject to the means test required for social assistance, to adequate benefits out of social assistance funds.

6. Where cash benefits provided under compulsory social insurance are based on previous earnings, they shall be at a rate of not less than two-thirds of the woman's previous earnings taken into account for the purpose of computing benefits.

7. Any contribution due under a compulsory social insurance scheme providing maternity benefits and any tax based upon payrolls which is raised for the purpose of providing such benefits shall, whether paid both by the employer and the employees or by the employer, be paid in respect of the total number of men and women employed by the undertakings concerned, without distinction of sex.

8. In no case shall the employer be individually liable for the cost of such benefits due to women employed by him.

Article 5

1. If a woman is nursing her child she shall be entitled to interrupt her work for this purpose at a time or times to be prescribed by national laws or regulations.

2. Interruptions of work for the purpose of nursing are to be counted as working hours and remunerated accordingly in cases in which the matter is governed by or in accordance with laws and regulations; in cases in which the matter is governed by collective agreement, the position shall be as determined by the relevant agreement.

Article 6

While a woman is absent from work on maternity leave in accordance with the provisions of Article 3 of this Convention, it shall not be lawful for her employer to give her notice of dismissal during such absence, or to give her notice of dismissal at such a time that the notice would expire during such absence.

Article 7

1. Any Member of the International Labour Organisation which ratifies this Convention may, by a declaration accom-

panying its ratification, provide for exceptions from the application of the Convention in respect of—

(a) certain categories of non-industrial occupations;

(b) occupations carried on in agricultural undertakings, other than plantations;

(c) domestic work for wages in private households;

(d) women wage earners working at home;

(e) undertakings engaged in the transport of passengers or goods by sea.

2. The categories of occupations or undertakings in respect of which the Member proposes to have recourse to the provisions of paragraph 1 of this Article shall be specified in the declaration accompanying its ratification.

3. Any Member which has made such a declaration may at any time cancel that declaration, in whole or in part, by a subsequent declaration.

4. Any Member for which a declaration made under paragraph 1 of this Article is in force shall indicate each year in its annual report upon the application of this Convention the position of its law and practice in respect of the occupations or undertakings to which paragraph 1 of this Article applies in virtue of the said declaration and the extent to which effect has been given or is proposed to be given to the Convention in respect of such occupations or undertakings.

5. At the expiration of five years from the first entry into force of this Convention, the Governing Body of the International Labour Offce shall submit to the Conference a special report concerning the application of these exceptions, containing such proposals as it may think appropriate for further action in regard to the matter.

Article 8

The formal ratifications of this Convention shall be communicated to the Director-General of the International Labour Office for registration.

Article 9

1. This Convention shall be binding only upon those Members of the International Labour Organisation whose ratifications have been registered with the Director-General.

2. It shall come into force twelve months after the date on which the ratifications of two Members have been registered with the Director-General.

3. Thereafter, this Convention shall come into force for any Member twelve months after the date on which its ratification has been registered.

Article 10

1. Declarations communicated to the Director-General of the International Labour Office in accordance with paragraph 2 of Article 35 of the Constitution of the International Labour Organisation shall indicate—

(a) the territories in respect of which the Member concerned undertakes that the provisions of the Convention shall be applied without modification;

(b) the territories in respect of which it undertakes that the provisions of the Convention shall be applied subject to modifications, together with details of the said modifications;

(c) the territories in respect of which the Convention is inapplicable and in such cases the grounds on which it is inapplicable;

(d) the territories in respect of which it reserves its decision pending further consideration of the position.

2. The undertakings referred to in subparagraphs *(a)* and *(b)* of paragraph 1 of this Article shall be deemed to be an integral part of the ratification and shall have the force of ratification.

3. Any Member may at any time by a subsequent declaration cancel in whole or in part any reservation made in its

original declaration in virtue of subparagraphs *(b)*, *(c)* or *(d)* of paragraph 1 of this Article.

4. Any Member may, at any time at which the Convention is subject to denunciation in accordance with the provisions of Article 12, communicate to the Director-General a declaration modifying in any other respect the terms of any former declaration and stating the present position in respect of such territories as it may specify.

Article 11

1. Declarations communicated to the Director-General of the International Labour Office in accordance with paragraphs 4 or 5 of Article 35 of the Constitution of the International Labour Organisation shall indicate whether the provisions of the Convention will be applied in the territory concerned without modification or subject to modifications; when the declaration indicates that the provisions of the Conventions will be applied subject to modifications, it shall give details of the said modifications.

2. The Member, Members or international authority concerned may at any time by a subsequent declaration renounce in whole or in part the right to have recourse to any modification indicated in any former declaration.

3. The Member, Members or international authority concerned may, at any time at which this Convention is subject to denunciation in accordance with the provisions of Article 12, communicate to the Director-General a declaration modifying in any other respect the terms of any former declaration and stating the present position in respect of the application of the Convention.

Article 12

1. A Member which has ratified this Convention may denounce it after the expiration of ten years from the date on which the Convention first comes into force, by an act communicated to the Director-General of the International Labour

Office for registration. Such denunciation shall not take effect until one year after the date on which it is registered.

2. Each Member which has ratified this Convention and which does not, within the year following the expiration of the period of ten years mentioned in the preceding paragraph, exercise the right of denunciation provided for in this Article, will be bound for another period of ten years and, thereafter, may denounce this Convention at the expiration of each period of ten years under the terms provided for in this Article.

Article 13

1. The Director-General of the International Labour Office shall notify all Members of the International Labour Organisation of the registration of all ratifications, declarations and denunciations communicated to him by the Members of the Organisation.

2. When notifying the Members of the Organisations of the registration of the second ratification communicated to him, the Director-General shall draw the attention of the Members of the Organisation to the date upon which the Convention will come into force.

Article 14

The Director-General of the International Labour Office shall communicate to the Secretary-General of the United Nations for registration in accordance with Article 102 of the Charter of the United Nations full particulars of all ratifications, declarations and acts of denunciation registered by him in accordance with the provisions of the preceding Articles.

Article 15

At such times as it may consider necessary the Governing Body of the International Labour Office shall present to the General Conference a report on the working of this Convention and shall examine the desirability of placing on the agenda of the Conference the question of its revision in whole or in part.

Article 16

1. Should the Conference adopt a new Convention revising this convention in whole or in part, then, unless the new Convention otherwise provides—

(a) the ratification by a Member of the new revising Convention shall *ipso jure* involve the immediate denunciation of this Convention, notwithstanding the provisions of Article 12 above, if and when the new revising Convention shall have come into force;

(b) as from the date when the new revising Convention comes into force this Convention shall cease to be open to ratification by the Members.

2. This Convention shall in any case remain in force in its actual form and content for those Members which have ratified it but have not ratified the revising Convention.

Article 17

The English and French versions of the text of this Convention are equally authoritative.

Recommendation (No. 95) Concerning Maternity Protection

The General Conference of the International Labour Organisation,

> Having been convened at Geneva by the Governing Body of the International Labour Office, and having met in its Thirty-fifth Session on 4 June 1952, and

> Having decided upon the adoption of certain proposals with regard to maternity protection, which is the seventh item on the agenda of the session, and

> Having determined that these proposals shall take the form of a Recommendation supplementing the Maternity Protection Convention (Revised), 1952,

adopts this twenty-eighth day of June of the year one thousand nine hundred and fifty-two the following Recommendation, which may be cited as the Maternity Protection Recommendation, 1952.

I. Maternity Leave

1. (1) Where necessary to the health of the woman and wherever practicable, the maternity leave provided for in Article 3, paragraph 2, of the Maternity Protection Convention (Revised), 1952, should be extended to a total period of 14 weeks.

(2) The supervisory bodies should have power to prescribe in individual cases, on the basis of a medical certificate, a further extension of the ante-natal and post-natal leave provided for in paragraphs 4, 5, and 6, or Article 3 of the Maternity Protection Convention (Revised), 1952, if such an extension seems necessary for safeguarding the health of the mother and the child, and, in particular, in the event of actual or threatening abnormal conditions, such as miscarriage and other ante-natal and post-natal complications.

II. *Maternity Benefits*

2. (1) Wherever practicable the cash benefits to be granted in conformity with Article 4 of the Maternity Protection Convention (Revised), 1952, should be fixed at a higher rate than the minimum standard provided in the Convention, equalling, where practicable, 100 per cent of the woman's previous earnings taken into account for the purpose of computing benefits.

(2) Wherever practicable the medical benefits to be granted in conformity with Article 4 of the said Convention should comprise general practitioner and specialist out-patient and in-patient care, including domiciliary visiting; dental care; the care given by qualified midwives and other maternity services at home or in hospital; nursing care at home or in hospital or other medical institutions; maintenance in hospitals or other medical institutions; pharmaceutical, dental or other medical or surgical supplies; and the care furnished under appropriate medical supervision by members of such other professions as may at any time be legally recognised as competent to furnish services associated with maternity care.

(3) The medical benefit should be afforded with a view to maintaining, restoring or improving the health of the woman protected and her ability to work and to attend to her personal needs.

(4) The institutions or government departments administering the medical benefit should encourage the women protected, by such means as may be deemed appropriate, to avail themselves of the general health services placed at their disposal by the public authorities or by other bodies recognised by the public authorities.

(5) In addition, national laws or regulations may authorise such institutions or government departments to make provision for the promotion of the health of the women protected and their infants.

(6) Other benefits in kind or in cash, such as layettes or payment for the purchase of layettes, the supply of milk or

of nursing allowance for nursing mothers, etc., might be usefully added to the benefits mentioned in subparagraphs (1) and (2) of this paragraph.

III. Facilities for Nursing Mothers and Infants

3. (1) Wherever practicable nursing breaks should be extended to a total period of at least one-and-a-half hours during the working day and adjustments in the frequency and length of the nursing periods should be permitted on production of a medical certificate.

(2) Provision should be made for the establishment of facilities for nursing or day care, preferably outside the undertakings where the women are working; wherever possible provision should be made for the financing or at least subsidising of such facilities at the expense of the community or by compulsory social insurance.

(3) The equipment and hygienic requirements of the facilities for nursing and day care and the number and qualifications of the staff of the latter should comply with adequate standards laid down by appropriate regulations, and they should be approved and supervised by the competent authority.

IV. Protection of Employment

4. (1) Wherever possible the period before and after confinement during which the woman is protected from dismissal by the employer in accordance with Article 6 of the Maternity Protection Convention (Revised), 1952, should be extended to begin as from the date when the employer of the woman has been notified by medical certificate of her pregnancy and to continue until one month at least after the end of the period of maternity leave provided for in Article 3 of the Convention.

(2) Among the legitimate reasons for dismissal during the protected period to be defined by law should be included cases of serious fault on the part of the employed woman, shutting down of the undertaking or expiry of the contract of

employment. Where works councils exist it would be desirable that they should be consulted regarding such dismissals.

(3) During her legal absence from work before and after confinement, the seniority rights of the woman should be preserved as well as her right to reinstatement in her former work or in equivalent work paid at the same rate.

V. Protection of the Health of Employed Women during the Maternity Period

5. (1) Night work and overtime work should be prohibited for pregnant and nursing women and their working hours should be planned so as to ensure adequate rest periods.

(2) Employment as a woman on work prejudicial to her health or that of her child, as defined by the competent authority, should be prohibited during pregnancy and up to at least three months after confinement and longer if the woman is nursing her child.

(3) Work falling under the provisions of subparagraph (2) should include, in particular—

(a) any hard labour involving—
   (i) heavy weight-lifting, pulling or pushing; or
   (ii) undue and unaccustomed physical strain, including prolonged standing;

(b) work requiring special equilibrium; and

(c) work with vibrating machines.

(4) A woman ordinarily employed at work defined as prejudicial to health by the competent authority should be entitled without loss of wages to a transfer to another kind of work not harmful to her health.

(5) Such a right of transfer should also be given for reasons of maternity in individual cases to any woman who presents a medical certificate stating that a change in the nature of her work is necessary in the interest of her health and that of her child.

Convention (No. 111) Concerning Discrimination in Respect of Employment and Occupation

[Vol. 362 U.N.T.S., p. 32]

Editor's Comments. *An ILO convention which has some of the broadest bearing on the rights of women is the Convention Concerning Discrimination in Respect of Employment Occupation, also known as the Discrimination (Employment and Occupation) Convention.*[9] *Adopted on June 25, 1958, this convention's achievement may be summed up in three main areas: a general undertaking by its signatories, some methods by which those undertakings may be given effect, and a statement of principle which provides for exceptions to the fundamental aim of the treaty.*

In case of the first area, each state undertakes to declare and pursue *national policies designed to promote, by means compatible with its national conditions and practices, equality of "opportunity and treatment in respect of employment and occupation." Such national policies should have the goal of "eliminating any discrimination" relating to employment and occupation. And, Article 1 of the convention defines the term "discrimination" as including "any distinction, exclusion or preference" made on the basis, of among other things, sex, and which has the "effect of nullifying or impairing equality of opportunity or treatment in employment occupation."*

How might this be achieved? Article 3 of the convention says that states may enact legislation and promote programs likely to secure the acceptance and observance of the sought employment policies or plans. The pursuit of those measures should be under the direct control of the national government. *This brings us to the principle of exception.*

The basic end which the convention seeks to achieve is a general prohibition against discrimination. But Article 5 takes the position that special measures of assistance or protection provided by other ILO treaties or recommendations are not to be viewed as discrimination. And that action by member countries are not discriminatory if, "after consultation with employers' and workers' organizations ... (they) determine that ... special measures (are needed) to meet particular requirements of persons who, for reasons such as sex ... are generally recognized to require special protection or assistance. "[10]

On that very day that the convention under discussion was adopted by the ILO, the organization also adopted, as a complement to the convention, a Recommendation Concerning Discrimination in Respect of Employment Occupation. That recommendation, which follows the text of the convention, provides some rather detailed suggestions about how government may go about creating and implementing national policies against employment discrimination.

The convention, ratified by over a hundred nation-states, came into force on October 15, 1960. The full text follows.

The General Conference of the International Labour Organisation,

Having been convened at Geneva by the Governing Body of the International Labour Office, and having met in its Forty-second Session on 4 June 1958, and

Having decided upon the adoption of certain proposals with regard to discrimination in the field of employment and occupation, which is the fourth item on the agenda of the session, and

Having determined that these proposals shall take the form of an international Convention, and

Considering that the Declaration of Philadelphia affirms that all human beings, irrespective of race, creed or sex, have the right to pursue both their material well-being and their spiritual development in conditions of freedom and dignity, of economic security and equal opportunity, and

Considering further that discrimination constitutes a violation of rights enunciated by the Universal Declaration of Human Rights,

adopts this twenty-fifth day of June of the year one thousand nine hundred and fifty-eight the following Convention, which may be cited as the Discrimination (Employment and Occupation) Convention, 1958:

Article 1

1. For the purpose of this Convention the term "discrimination" includes—

(a) any distinction, exclusion or preference made on the basis of race, colour, sex, religion, political opinion, national extraction or social origin, which has the effect of nullifying or impairing equality of opportunity or treatment in employment or occupation;

(b) such other distinction, exclusion or preference which has the effect of nullifying or impairing equality of opportunity or treatment in employment or occupation as may be determined by the Member concerned after consultation with representative employers' and workers' organisations, where such exist, and with other appropriate bodies.

2. Any distinction, exclusion or preference in respect of a particular job based on the inherent requirements thereof shall not be deemed to be discrimination.

3. For the purpose of this Convention the terms "employment" and "occupation" include access to vocational training, access to employment and to particular occupations, and terms and conditions of employment.

Article 2

Each Member for which this Convention is in force undertakes to declare and pursue a national policy designed to promote, by methods appropriate to national conditions and practice, equality of opportunity and treatment in respect of employment and occupation, with a view to eliminating any discrimination in respect thereof.

Article 3

Each Member for which this Convention is in force undertakes, by methods appropriate to national conditions and practice —

(a) to seek the co-operation of employers' and workers' organisation and other appropriate bodies in promoting the acceptance and observance of this policy;

(b) to enact such legislation and to promote such educational programmes as may be calculated to secure the acceptance and observance of the policy;

(c) to repeal any statutory provisions and modify any administrative instructions or practices which are inconsistent with the policy;

(d) to pursue the policy in respect of employment under the direct control of a national authority;

(e) to ensure observance of the policy in the activities of vocational guidance, vocational training and placement services under the direction of a national authority;

(f) to indicate in its annual reports on the application of the Convention the action taken in pursuance of the policy and the results secured by such action.

Article 4

Any measures affecting an individual who is justifiably suspected of, or engaged in, activities prejudicial to the security of the State shall not be deemed to be discrimination, provided that the individual concerned shall have the right to appeal to a competent body established in accordance with national practice.

Article 5

1. Special measures of protection or assistance provided for in other conventions or Recommendations adopted by the International Labour Conference shall not be deemed to be discrimination.

2. Any Member may, after consultation with representative employers' and workers' organisations, where such exist, determine that other special measures designed to meet the particular requirements of persons who, for reasons such as sex, age, disablement, family responsibilities or social or cultural status, are generally recognised to require special protection or assistance, shall not be deemed to be discrimination.

Article 6

Each Member which ratifies this Convention undertakes to apply it to non-metropolitan territories in accordance with the provisions of the Constitution of the International Labour Organisation.

Article 7

The formal ratifications of this Convention shall be communicated to the Director-General of the International Labour Office for registration.

Article 8

1. This Convention shall be binding only upon those Members of the International Labour Organisation whose ratifications have been registered with the Director-General.

2. It shall come into force twelve months after the date on which the ratifications of two Members have been registered with the Director-General.

3. Thereafter, this Convention shall come into force for any Member twelve months after the date on which its ratification has been registered.

Article 9

1. A Member which has ratified this Convention may denounce it after the expiration of ten years from the date on which the Convention first comes into force by an act communicated to the Director-General of the International Labour Office

for registration. Such denunciation shall not take effect until one year after the date on which it is registered.

2. Each member which has ratified this Convention and which does not, within the year following the expiration of the period of ten years mentioned in the preceding paragraph, exercise the right of denunciation provided for in this Article, will be bound for another period of ten years and, thereafter, may denounce this Convention at the expiration of each period of ten years under the terms provided for in this Article.

Article 10

1. The Director-General of the International Labour Office shall notify all Members of the International Labour Organisation of the registration of all ratifications and denunciations communicated to him by the Members of the Organisation.

2. When notifying the Members of the Organisation of the registration of the second ratification communicated to him, the Director-General shall draw the attention of the Members of the Organisation to the date upon which the Convention will come into force.

Article 11

The Director-General of the International Labour Office shall communicate to the Secretary-General of the United Nations for registration in accordance with Article 102 of the Charter of the United Nations full particulars of all ratifications and acts of denunciation registered by him in accordance with the provisions of the preceding Articles.

Article 12

At such times as it may consider necessary the Governing Body of the International Labour Office shall present to the General Conference a report on the working of this Convention and shall examine the desirability of placing on the agenda of the Conference the question of its revision in whole or in part.

Article 13

1. Should the Conference adopt a new Convention revising this Convention in whole or in part, then, unless the new Convention otherwise provides—

(a) the ratification by a Member of the new revising Convention shall *ipso jure* involve the immediate denunciation of this Convention, notwithstanding the provisions of Article 9 above, if and when the new revising Convention shall have come into force;

(b) as from the date when the new revising Convention comes into force this Convention shall cease to be open to ratification by the Members.

2. This Convention shall in any case remain in force in its actual form and content for those Members which have ratified it but have not ratified the revising Convention.

Article 14

The English and French versions of the text of this Convention are equally authoritative.

Recommendation (No. 111) Concerning Discrimination in Respect of Employment and Occupation

The General Conference of the International Labour Organisation,

> Having been convened at Geneva by the Governing Body of the International Labour Office, and having met in its Forty-second Session on 4 June 1958, and

> Having decided upon the adoption of certain proposals with regard to discrimination in the field of employment and occupation, which is the fourth item on the agenda of the session, and

> Having determined that these proposals shall take the form of a recommendation supplementing the Discrimination (Employment and Occupation) Convention, 1958,

adopts this twenty-fifth day of June of the year one thousand nine hundred and fifty-eight the following Recommendation, which may be cited as the Discrimination (Employment and Occupation) Recommendation, 1958:

The Conference recommends that each Member should apply the following provisions:

I. Definitions

1. (1) For the purpose of this Recommendation the term "discrimination" includes—

(a) any distinction, exclusion or preference made on the basis of race, colour, sex, religion, political opinion, national extraction or social origin, which has the effect of nullifying or impairing equality of opportunity or treatment in employment or occupation;

(b) such other distinction, exclusion or preference which has the effect of nullifying or impairing equality of opportunity or treatment in employment or occupation as may be determined by the Member concerned after consultation with representative employers' and workers' organisations, where such exist, and with other appropriate bodies.

(2) Any distinction, exclusion or preference in respect of a particular job based on the inherent requirements thereof is not deemed to be discrimination.

(3) For the purpose of this Recommendation the terms "employment" and "occupation" include access to vocational training, access to employment and to particular occupations, and terms and conditions of employment.

II. *Formulation and Application of Policy*

2. Each Member should formulate a national policy for the prevention of discrimination in employment and occupation. This policy should be applied by means of legislative measures, collective agreements between representative employers' and workers' organisations or in any other manner consistent with national conditions and practice, and should have regard to the following principles:

(a) the promotion of equality of opportunity and treatment in employment and occupation is a matter of public concern;

(b) all persons should, without discrimination, enjoy equality of opportunity and treatment in respect of—

    (i) access to vocational guidance and placement services;

    (ii) access to training and employment of their own choice on the basis of individual suitability for such training or employment;

    (iii) advancement in accordance with their individual character, experience, ability and diligence;

    (iv) security of tenure of employment;

    (v) remuneration for work of equal value;

    (vi) conditions of work including hours of work, rest periods, annual holidays with pay, occupational safety and occupational health measures, as well as social security measures and welfare facilities and benefits provided in connection with employment;

(c) government agencies should apply non-discriminatory employment policies in all their activities;

(d) employers should not practise or countenance discrimination in engaging or training any person for employment, in advancing or retaining such person in employment, or in fixing terms and conditions of employment; nor should any person or organisation obstruct or interfere, either directly or indirectly, with employers in pursuing this principle;

(e) in collective negotiations and industrial relations the parties should respect the principle of equality of opportunity and treatment in employment and ocupation, and should ensure that collective agreements contain no provisions of a discriminatory character in respect of access to, training for, advancement in or retention of employment or in respect of the terms and conditions of employment;

(f) employers' and workers' organisations should not practise or countenance discrimination in respect of admission, retention of membership or participation in their affairs.

3. Each Member should—

(a) ensure application of the principles of non-discrimination—

    (i) in respect of employment under the direct control of a national authority;

    (ii) in the activities of vocational guidance, vocational training and placement services under the direction of a national authority;

(b) promote their observance, where practicable and necessary, in respect of other employment and other vocational guidance, vocational training and placement services by such methods as—

    (i) encouraging state, provincial or local government departments or agencies and industries and undertakings operated under public ownership or control to ensure the application of the principles;

    (ii) making eligibility for contracts involving the

expenditure of public funds dependent on observance of the principles;

(iii) making eligibility for grants to training establishments and for a licence to operate a private employment agency or a private vocational guidance office dependent on observance of the principles.

4. Appropriate agencies, to be assisted where practicable by advisory committees composed of representatives of employers' and workers' organisations, where such exist, and of other interested bodies, should be established for the purpose of promoting application of the policy in all fields of public and private employment, and in particular—

(a) to take all practicable measures to foster public understanding an acceptance of the principles of non-discrimination;

(b) to receive, examine and investigate complaints that the policy is not being observed and, if necessary by conciliation, to secure the correction of any practice regarded as in conflict with the policy; and

(c) to consider further any complaints which cannot be effectively settled by conciliation and to render opinions or issue decisions concerning the manner in which discriminatory practices revealed should be corrected.

5. Each Member should repeal any statutory provisions and modify any administrative instructions or practices which are inconsistent with the policy.

6. Application of the policy should not adversely affect special measures designed to meet the particular requirements of persons who, for reasons such as sex, age, disablement, family responsibilities or social or cultural status are generally recognised to require special protection or assistance.

7. Any measures affecting an individual who is justifiably suspected of, or engaged in, activities prejudicial to the security of the State should not be deemed to be discrimination, provided that the individual concerned has the right to appeal to a competent body established in accordance with national practice.

8. With respect to immigrant workers of foreign nationality and the members of their families, regard should be had to the provisions of the Migration for Employment Convention (Revised), 1949, relating to equality of treatment and the provisions of the Migration for Employment Recommendation (Revised), 1949, relating to the lifting of restrictions on access to employment.

9. There should be continuing co-operation between the competent authorities, representatives of employers and workers and appropriate bodies to consider what further positive measures may be necessary in the light of national conditions to put the principles of non-discrimination into effect.

III. Co-Ordination of Measures for the Prevention of Discrimination in All Fields

10. The authorities responsible for action against discrimination in employment and occupation should co-operate closely and continuously with the authorities responsible for action against discrimination in other fields in order that measures taken in all fields may be co-ordinated.

Convention Against Discrimination in Education

[Vol. 429 U.N.T.S., p. 93]

Editor's Comments. *The last treaty in this portion of the volume is the Convention Against Discrimination in Education, adopted by UNESCO on December 14, 1960. This convention, its name misrepresenting somewhat its true character, is not only—as its title implies—about prohibiting discrimination in education; it is concerned as well with the promotion of equality in that field. Likewise, the treaty focuses on the* quality *of education that is to be made available.*

Taking its inspiration from the UDHR,[11] the convention declares education to be a right and requires states (a) to provide free and compulsory primary education, (b) to make secondary education, in all its variety, generally available *and* accessible *to all, and (c) to ensure that higher eduction is equally accessible to everyone. Further, all* public *educational institutions at the "same level" must have equivalent standards of education. Private schools are allowed, if they do not seek to exclude any group. Separate academic institutions for students of different sex are not regarded as discriminatory if they have equally qualified staff, equivalent premises and equipment of the same quality.*

The convention defines discrimination as, among other things, any "distinction, exclusion, limitation or preference . . . based on . . . sex"[12] and includes as acts of discrimination the limiting of any person or group to an education of inferior standard, depriving that person or group access to "education of any type or at any level," and inflicting on them conditions that are incompatible with their dignity. Particularly important to women's rights is the requirement that "in order to eliminate and prevent discrimination," states undertake to repeal any statutory measures or administrative practices that are educationally discriminatory.

The emphasis given to making secondary education in all its forms available and accessible to women is of utmost importance. First, it is still relatively common in many parts of the world, including the West, to have boys and girls exposed to significantly different curricula and orientation, despite the progress made toward coeducation. Second, if women are to have equal access to higher education, the "easy conscience" that allows parents and governments to "sacrifice" girls (when the cost of secondary education becomes burdensome) by steering them to less expensive schools must stop. A solid academic foundation at the secondary level is a prerequisite for equal access at the higher education level. Third, it is the principal means by which girls can prepare to fight discrimination in employment occupation and prepare for full "participation in the productive life of their communities and nations."[13] Finally, it is not only an instrument by which even "enlightened men" may help to divest themselves of the more subtle discriminatory attitudes against women,[14] but the source through which women may begin to experience the full flowering of their personalities.

The convention came into force on May 22, 1962. The full text follows.

The General Conference of the United Nations Educational, Scientific and Cultural Organisation, meeting in Paris from 14 November to 14 December 1960, at its eleventh session,

> Recalling that the Universal Declaration of Human Rights asserts the principle of non-discrimination and proclaims that every person has the right to education,

> Considering that, discrimination in education is a violation of rights enunciated in that Declaration,

> Considering that, under the terms of its Constitution, the United Nations Educational, Scientific and Cultural Organization has the purpose of instituting collaboration among the nations with a view to furthering for all universal respect for human rights and equality of educational opportunity,

> Recognizing that, consequently, the United Nations Educational, Scientific and Cultural Organization, while respecting the diversity of national educational systems,

has the duty not only to proscribe any form of discrimination in education but also to promote equality of opportunity and treatment for all in education,

Having before it proposals concerning the different aspects of discrimination in education, constituting item 17.1.4 of the agenda of the session,

Having decided at its tenth session that this question should be made the subject of an international convention as well as of recommendations to Member States,

adopts this Convention on the fourteenth day of December 1960.

Article 1

1. For the purposes of this Convention, the term "discrimination" includes any distinction, exclusion, limitation or preference which, being based on race, colour, sex, language, religion, political or other opinion, national or social origin, economic condition or birth, has the purpose or effect of nullifying or impairing equality of treatment in education and in particular:

(a) of depriving any person or group of persons of access to education of any type or at any level;

(b) of limiting any person or group of persons to education of an inferior standard;

(c) subject to the provisions of Article 2 of this Convention, of establishing or maintaining separate educational systems or institutions for persons or groups of persons; or

(d) of inflicting on any person or group of persons conditions which are incompatible with the dignity of man.

2. For the purposes of this Convention, the term "education" refers to all types and levels of education, and includes access to education, the standard and quality of education, and the conditions under which it is given.

Article 2

When permitted in a State, the following situations shall not be deemed to constitute discrimination, within the meaning of Article 1 of this Convention:

(a) the establishment or maintenance of separate educational systems or institutions for pupils of the two sexes, if these systems or institutions offer equivalent access to education, provide a teaching staff with qualifications of the same standard as well as school premises and equipment of the same quality, and afford the opportunity to take the same or equivalent courses of study;

(b) the establishment or maintenance, for religious or linguistic reasons, of separate educational systems or institutions offering an education which is in keeping with the wishes of the pupil's parents or legal guardians, if participation in such systems or attendance at such institutions is optional and if the education provided conforms to such standards as may be laid down or approved by the competent authorities, in particular for education of the same level;

(c) the establishment or maintenance of private educational institutions, if the object of the institutions is not to secure the exclusion of any group but to provide educational facilities in addition to those provided by the public authorities, if the institutions are conducted in accordance with that object, and if the education provided conforms with such standards as may be laid down or approved by the competent authorities, in particular for education of the same level.

Article 3

In order to eliminate and prevent discrimination within the meaning of this Convention, the States Parties thereto undertake:

(a) to abrogate any statutory provisions and any administrative instructions and to discontinue any administrative practices which involve discrimination in education;

(b) to ensure, by legislation where necessary, that there is no discrimination in the admission of pupils to educational institutions;

(c) not to allow any differences of treatment by the public authorities between nationals, except on the basis of merit or need, in the matter of school fees and the grant of scholarships or other forms of assistance to pupils and necessary permits and facilities for the pursuit of studies in foreign countries;

(d) not to allow, in any form of assistance granted by the public authorities to educational institutions, any restrictions or preference based solely on the ground that pupils belong to a particular group;

(e) to give foreign nationals resident within their territory the same access to education as that given to their own nationals.

Article 4

The States Parties to the Convention undertake furthermore to formulate, develop and apply a national policy which, by methods appropriate to the circumstances and to national usage, will tend to promote equality of opportunity and of treatment in the matter of education and in particular:

(a) to make primary education free and compulsory; make secondary education in its different forms generally available and accessible to all; make higher education equally accessible to all on the basis of individual capacity; assure compliance by all with the obligation to attend school prescribed by law;

(b) to ensure that the standards of education are equivalent in all public educational institutions of the same level, and that the conditions relating to the quality of the education provided are also equivalent;

(c) to encourage and intensify by appropriate methods the education of persons who have not received any primary education or who have not completed the entire primary

education course and the continuation of their education on the basis of individual capacity;

(*d*) to provide training for the teaching profession without discrimination.

Article 5

1. The States Parties to this Convention agree that:

(*a*) education shall be directed to the full development of the human personality and to the strengthening of respect for human rights and fundamental freedoms; it shall promote understanding, tolerance and friendship among all nations, racial or religious groups, and shall further the activities of the United Nations for the maintenance of peace;

(*b*) it is essential to respect the liberty of parents and, where applicable, of legal guardians, firstly to choose for their children institutions other than those maintained by the public authorities but conforming to such minimum educational standards as may be laid down or approved by the competent authorities and, secondly, to ensure in a manner consistent with the procedures followed in the State for the application of its legislation, the religious and moral education of the children in conformity with their own convictions; and no person or group of persons should be compelled to receive religious instruction inconsistent with his or their conviction;

(*c*) it is essential to recognize the right of members of national minorities to carry on their own educational activities, including the maintenance of schools and, depending on the educational policy of each State, the use or the teaching of their own language, provided however:

(i) that this right is not exercised in a manner which prevents the members of these minorities from understanding the culture and language of the community as a whole and from participating in its activities, or which prejudices national sovereignty;

(ii) that the standard of education is not lower than the

general standard laid down or approved by the competent authorities; and

(iii) that attendance at such schools is optional.

2. The States Parties to this Convention undertake to take all necessary measures to ensure the application of the principles enunciated in paragraph 1 of this Article.

Article 6

In the application of this Convention, the States Parties to it undertake to pay the greatest attention to any recommendations hereafter adopted by the General Conference of the United Nations Educational, Scientific and Cultural Organization defining the measures to be taken against the different forms of discrimination in education and for the purpose of ensuring equality of opportunity and treatment in education.

Article 7

The States Parties to this Convention shall in their periodic reports submitted to the General Conference of the United Nations Educational, Scientific and Cultural Organization on dates and in a manner to be determined by it, give information on the legislative and administrative provisions which they have adopted and other action which they have taken for the application of this convention, including that taken for the formulation and the development of the national policy defined in Article 4 as well as the results achieved and the obstacles encountered in the application of that policy.

Article 8

Any dispute which may arise between any two or more States Parties to this convention concerning the interpretation or application of this convention, which is not settled by negotiation shall at the request of the parties to the dispute be referred, failing other means of settling the dispute, to the International Court of Justice for decision.

Article 9

Reservations to the convention shall not be permitted.

Article 10

This Convention shall not have the effect of diminishing the rights which individuals or groups may enjoy by virtue of agreements concluded between two or more States, where such rights are not contrary to the letter or spirit of this Convention.

Article 11

This Convention is drawn up in English, French, Russian and Spanish, the four texts being equally authoritative.

Article 12

1. This Convention shall be subject to ratification or acceptance by States Members of the United Nations Educational, Scientific and Cultural Organization in accordance with their respective constitutional procedures.

2. The instruments of ratification or acceptance shall be deposited with the Director-General of the United Nations Educational, Scientific and Cultural Organization.

Article 13

1. This Convention shall be open to accession by all States not Members of the United Nations Educational, Scientific and Cultural Organization which are invited to do so by the Executive Board of the Organization.

2. Accession shall be effected by the deposit of an instrument of accession with the Director-General of the United Nations Educational, Scientific and Cultural Organization.

Article 14

This Convention shall enter into force three months after the date of the deposit of the third instrument of ratification, acceptance or accession, but only with respect to those States which have deposited their respective instruments on or before that date. It shall enter into force with respect to any other State three months after the deposit of its instrument of ratification, acceptance or accession.

Article 15

The States Parties to the Convention recognize that the Convention is applicable not only to their metropolitan territory but also to all non-self-governing, trust, colonial and other territories for the international relations of which they are responsible; they undertake to consult, if necessary, the governments or other competent authorities of these territories on or before ratification, acceptance or accession with a view to securing the application of the Convention to those territories, and to notify the Director-General of the United Nations Educational, Scientific and Cultural Organization of the territories to which it is accordingly applied, the notification to take effect three months after the date of its receipt.

Article 16

1. Each State Party to this Convention may denounce the Convention on its own behalf or on behalf of any territory for whose international relations it is responsible.

2. The denunciation shall be notified by an instrument in writing, deposited with the Director-General of the United Nations Educational, Scientific and Cultural Organization.

3. The denunciation shall take effect twelve months after the receipt of the instrument of denunciation.

Article 17

The Director-General of the United Nations Educational, Scientific and Cultural Organization shall inform the States Members of the Organization, the States not members of the Organization which are referred to in Article 13, as well as the United Nations, of the deposit of all the instruments of ratification, acceptance and accession provided for in Articles 12 and 13, and of the notifications and denunciations provided for in Articles 15 and 16 respectively.

Article 18

1. This Convention may be revised by the General Conference of the United Nations Educational, Scientific and Cultural Organization. Any such revision shall, however, bind only the States which shall become Parties to the revising convention.

2. If the General Conference should adopt a new convention revising this Convention in whole or in part, then, unless the new convention otherwise provides, this Convention shall cease to be open to ratification, acceptance or accession as from the date on which the new revising convention enters into force.

Article 19

In conformity with Article 102 of the Charter of the United Nations, this Convention shall be registered with the Secretariat of the United Nations at the request of the Director-General of the United Nations Educational, Scientific and Cultural Organization.

Done in Paris, this fifteenth day of December 1960, in two authentic copies bearing the signatures of the President of the eleventh session of the General Conference and of the Director-General of the United Nations Educational, Scientific and Cultural Organization, which shall be deposited in the archives of the United Nations Educational, Scientific and Cultural Organization, and certified true copies of which shall be delivered to all the States referred to in Articles 12 and 13 as well as to the United Nations.

The foregoing is the authentic text of the Convention duly adopted by the General Conference of the United Nations Educational, Scientific and Cultural Organization during its eleventh session, which was held in Paris and declared closed the fifteenth day of December 1960.

III. Nationality

Nationality (generally used interchangeably with citizenship, although the two are not always the same) denotes a bond that links individuals with a nation-state; to be more precise, it is the name which defines a person's membership in a given state. As a member of a state, an individual normally can expect and in fact does enjoy the protection—domestic and international—of that state. On the other hand, if an individual lacks nationality, she or he is without protection if she or he is damaged or otherwise wronged by any government.[1] Without the bond of nationality no state will generally be disposed, not to mention willing, to champion her or his cause against the government that has committed the wrong.

Because of their varying demographic and other conditions, states have been left relatively free under international law to decide on whom they will or will not confer their nationality,[2] the conditions under which nationality may be gained, and even the circumstances by which it may be lost. Some states accord nationality to individuals born within their territory; this right of nationality is referred to as *jus soli* (law of the soil).[3] Other states confer nationality at birth only to individuals who are born of parents that are already nationals. This right of nationality is called *jus sanguinis* (law of the blood). In addition to the mode of conferring nationality based on facts associated with birth, states accept another—that of naturalization, the process by which nationals of one state may apply for and be granted the nationality of another.

It is through the naturalization process that women have been most frequently discriminated against. Even today, a woman who marries a national of another state can lose her nationality. (She would, of course, gain that of her husband. But it could be lost upon a divorce, by her husband's change of nationality, or through modifications in the legislation of her "new homeland.") Men who marry foreign nationals do not likewise suffer this threat of loss of nationality. The UDHR affirms that "everyone has a right to a nationality,"[4] but it does not say that individuals have a right to the nationality of a particular state. Hence, women have often found themselves stateless.

It is in part to correct this unequal treatment of women that the convention which follows was agreed on and adopted.

Convention on the Nationality
of Married Women
[Opened for signature and ratification by General
Assembly Resolution 1040 (XI) 29 January 1957]

Editor's Comments. *The issue of the nationality of
women has been a significant concern of the United Nations
since 1948. In past years, a study of the question by its Commission on the Status of Women (CSW) uncovered many and
varied expressions of discrimination against women—a
discrimination principally resulting from the conflicts of
nationality laws which nation-states created. The study also
reviewed and reflected on treaties, examinations, analyses,
deliberations or investigations which had been previously
engaged in, or developed by, other institutions including the
League of Nations. And, on the basis of its efforts, the CSW,
at its third session in 1949, expressed the view that a convention
on the nationality of married women should be promptly
prepared, assuring women equality with men in the exercise of
this right and, in particular, preventing women from becoming
stateless persons. This view was endorsed by the Economic
and Social Council (ECOSOC) in resolution 242 (IX) on
August 1, 1949.*

*In 1955, the commission completed the preparation of a
draft Convention on the Nationality of Married Women and
sent it to the ECOSOC which, in turn, approved and for-
warded it to the General Assembly for final approval. That
approval was received when the General Assembly adopted the
convention and opened it for signature, ratification and accession by resolution 1040 (XI) on January 29, 1957. The
convention came into force August 11, 1958.*

*The principal thrust of the convention may be said to be,
in the important matter of married women's nationality, the
establishment of the principle of equality between the sexes. But
it does more. It represents an important step in a development
which has been anticipated by the Hague Convention on
Certain questions Relating to the Conflict of Nationality Law
of 1930—a development which sought to replace the traditional*

principle of the "unity of the family" as "headed by husband" with the principle of independence of nationality of the wife from that of her husband. The full text follows.

Recognizing that, conflicts in law in practice with reference to nationality arise as a result of provisions concerning the loss or acquisition of nationality by women as a result of marriage, of its dissolution or of the change of nationality by the husband during marriage,

Recognizing that in Article 15 of the Universal Declaration Human Rights, the General Assembly of the United Nations has proclaimed that "everyone has the right to a nationality" and that "no one shall be arbitrarily deprived of his nationality nor denied the right to change his nationality,"

Desiring to cooperate with the United Nations in promoting universal respect for, and observance of, human rights and fundamental freedoms for all without distinction as to sex,

Hereby agree as hereinafter provided:

Article 1

Each Contracting State agrees that neither the celebration nor the dissolution of a marriage between one of its nationals and an alien, nor the change of nationality by the husband during marriage, shall automatically affect the nationality of the wife.

Article 2

Each Contracting State agrees that neither the voluntary acquisition of the nationality of another State nor the renunciation of its nationality by one of its nationals shall prevent the retention of its nationality by the wife of such national.

Article 3

1. Each Contracting State agrees that the alien wife of one of its nationals may, at her request, acquire the nationality of her

husband through specially privileged naturalization procedures; the grant of such nationality may be subject to such limitations as may be imposed in the interests of national security of public policy.

2. Each Contracting State agrees that the present Convention shall not be construed as affecting any legislation or judicial practice by which the alien wife of one of its nationals may, at her request, acquire her husband's nationality as a matter of right.

Article 4

1. The present Convention shall be open for signature and ratification on behalf of any State Member of the United Nations and also on behalf of any other State which is or hereafter becomes a member of any specialized agency of the United Nations, or which is or hereafter becomes a Party to the Statute of the International Court of Justice, or any other State to which an invitation has been addressed by the General Assembly of the United Nations.

2. The present convention shall be ratified and the instruments of ratification shall be deposited with the Secretary-General of the United Nations.

Article 5

1. The present Convention shall be open for accession to all States referred to in paragraph 1 of Article 4.

2. Accession shall be effected by the deposit of an instrument of accession with the Secretary-General of the United Nations.

Article 6

1. The present Convention shall come into force on the ninetieth day following the date of deposit of the sixth instrument of ratification or accession.

2. For each state ratifying or acceding to the Convention

after the deposit of the sixth instrument of ratification or accession, the Convention shall enter into force on the ninetieth day after deposit by such State of its instrument of ratification or accession.

Article 7

1. The present Convention shall apply to all non-self-governing, trust, colonial and other non-metropolitan territories for the international relations of which any Contracting State is responsible; the Contracting State concerned shall, subject to the provisions of paragraph 2 of the present article, at the time of signature, ratification or accession declare the non-metropolitan territory or territories to which the Convention shall apply *ipso facto* as a result of such signature, ratification or accession.

2. In any case in which, for the purpose of nationality, a non-metropolitan territory, is not treated as one with the metropolitan territory, or in any case in which the previous consent of a non-metropolitan territory is required by the constitutional laws or practices of the Contracting State or of the non-metropolitan territory for the application of the Convention to that territory, that Contracting State shall endeavour to secure the needed consent of the non-metropolitan territory within the period of twelve months from the date of signature of the Convention by that Contracting State, and when such consent has been obtained the Contracting State shall notify the Secretary-General of the United Nations. The present Convention shall apply to the territory or territories named in such notification from the date of its receipt by the Secretary-General.

3. After the expiry of the twelve-month period mentioned in paragraph 2 of the present article, the Contracting States concerned shall inform the Secretary-General of the results of the consultations with those non-metropolitan territories for whose international relations they are responsible and whose consent to the application of the present Convention may have been withheld.

Article 8

1. At the time of signature, ratification or accession, any State may make reservations to any article of the present Convention other than Articles 1 and 2.

2. If any State makes a reservation in accordance with paragraph 1 of the present article, the Convention, with the exception of those provisions to which the reservation relates, shall have effect as between the reserving State and the other Parties. The Secretary-General of the United Nations shall communicate the text of the reservation to all States which are or may become Parties to the Convention. Any State Party to the Convention or which thereafter becomes a Party may notify the Secretary-General that it does not agree to consider itself bound by the Convention with respect to the State making the reservation. This notification must be made in the case of a State already a Party, within ninety days from the date of the communication by the Secretary-General; and, in the case of a State subsequently becoming a Party within ninety days from the date when the instrument of ratification or accession is deposited. In the event that such a notification is made, the Convention shall not be deemed to be in effect as between the State making the notification and the State making the reservation.

3. Any State making a reservation in accordance with paragraph 1 of the present article may at any time withdraw the rservation, in whole or in part, after it has been accepted, by a notification to this effect addressed to the Secretary-General of the United Nations. Such notification shall take effect on the date on which it is received.

Article 9

1. Any Contracting State may denounce the present Convention by written notification to the Secretary-General of the United Nations. Denunciation shall take effect one year after the date of receipt of the notification by the Secretary-General.

2. The present Convention shall cease to be in force as from the date when the denunciation which reduces the number of Parties to less than six becomes effective.

Article 10

Any dispute which may arise between any two or more Contracting States concerning the interpretation or application of the present Convention which is not settled by negotiation, shall, at the request of any one of the Parties to the dispute, be referred to the International Court of Justice for decision, unless the Parties agree to another mode of settlement.

Article 11

The Secretary-General of the United Nations shall notify all States Members of the United Nations and the non-member States contemplated in paragraph 1 of Article 4 of the present Convention of the following:

(a) signatures and instruments of ratification received in accordance with Article 4;

(b) instruments of accession received in accordance with Article 5;

(c) the date upon which the present Convention enters into force in accordance with Article 6;

(d) communications and notifications received in accordance with Article 8;

(e) notifications of denunciation received in accordance with paragraph 1 of Article 9;

(f) abrogation in accordance with paragraph 2 of Article 9.

Article 12

1. The present Convention, of which the Chinese, English, French, Russian and Spanish texts shall be equally authentic, shall be deposited in the archives of the United Nations.

2. The Secretary-General of the United Nations shall transmit a certified copy of the Convention to all States Members of the United Nations and to the non-member States contemplated in paragraph 1 of Article 4.

IV. Marriage, Family and Children

The focus of this section on marriage, family, and children seems logical because of tradition, the composition of certain international agreements, and the contemporary fact that people throughout the world associate marriage with family and children. Indeed, from the standpoint of discrimination against women, the three are inseparable.

Tradition has linked the institution of marriage, formal or informal, to the social unit called the family. That tradition would, in fact, define marriage as an institution through which men and women are joined in a special kind of legal and social dependence for the *purpose* of founding and maintaining a family.[1] And, were one to investigate definitions of family, the most common one would be: the basic unit of society having as its members two or more adults living together and cooperating in the care and rearing of their own or adopted children.

This thinking influenced the outlook of those who had discussed and adopted many of the international agreements with which this work and modern nation-states have been concerned. Among these agreements is the UDHR, Article 16 which provides that "the family is the natural and fundamental group unit of society and entitled to protection by society and the state." The same article also recites that men and women of full age do not only have the right to marry but, as well, "to found a family." Surely, the international instruments under consideration in this section have been composed to reflect the thinking earlier referred to in this paragraph.

Our intellectual and moral constitution also makes the link among marriage, family and children. Worldwide, socialization has predisposed us to certain gender roles, shaped our assumptions about gender power and vulnerability, and helped to construct a number of social structures that define the very discrimination that women must fight. For example, the Declaration on the Protection of Women and Children in Emergency and Armed Conflict links women and children in common legal protection which may, in some instances, reflect a concern for the vulnerability of a pregnant woman. But it bespeaks much more. It points to, among other things, a culture that has not only assigned to women the primary responsibility for the physical, social and moral welfare of children, but, likewise, has presided over various aspects of women's social vulnerability. The last of the instruments in this section represents an attempt to reduce that vulnerability—at least, an effort to make men and women share aspects of it equally.

Convention on Consent to Marriage, Minimum Age for Marriage and Registration of Marriages
[Vol. 521 U.N.T.S., p. 231]

Editor's Comments. *The issues related to marriage and its role in the unequal status of women are many. These issues include the common requirement that the woman assume her husband's name and change her nationality as well as accept limitation on her right to contract, to sue or be sued, and to acquire, administer, enjoy or dispose of an interest in property. Another issue involves matters concerning denial of the right to give her consent to marriage itself. Girls of tender ages are "given away" in marriage. Many women are victims of polygamy, especially where registration of marriages is not required. Even in the "socially advanced" United States there are over a thousand laws that discriminate against women,[2] and one finds diplomatic wives systematically discriminated against. In fact, until 1971, a woman had to choose between marriage and the pursuit of a career in the diplomatic profession.[3] The reverse, of course, was never the case for men. It is no wonder that Blackstone in one of his more famous dicta saw marriage, in many senses, as a form of "civil death" for women.*

The convention here under consideration does not deal with all of the issues mentioned above. Many have been left to, among others, the Convention on the Elimination of All Discrimination Against Women, which will later follow. The Convention on the Consent to Marriage, Minimum Age for Marriage and Registration of Marriages, adopted by the General Assembly on December 10, 1962, seeks to ensure the equal rights of women and men "as to marriage, during marriage and at it dissolution" by virtue of the "principle of free consent to marriage" and by the prohibition of child marriages. The convention specifies in Article 1 that "no marriage shall be legally entered into without the full and free consent of both parties"; and that consent is to be expressed by "them in person after due publicity and in the presence of the authority" which, by law, is competent to solemnize marriages.

The convention also urges states to specify a minimum age

for marriage; and, although it does not suggest such an age, a 1965 recommendation by the General Assembly urges that 15 years be taken as a minimum age. It may also be instructive to note that at a 1956 U.N. conference dealing with slavery, the slave trade and other practices similar to slavery, it was urged that the question of a minimum age "preferably no less than fourteen years" be studied.[4] Likewise, the conference considered a study of the question of free consent of both parties to a marriage.

The convention came into force December 9, 1965. The full text follows.

Preamble

The Contracting States,

Desiring, in conformity with the Charter of the United Nations, to promote universal respect for, and observance of, human rights and fundamental freedoms for all, without distinction as to race, sex, language or religion,

Recalling that Article 16 of the Universal Declaration of Human Rights states that:

"(1) Men and women of full age, without any limitation due to race, nationality or religion, have the right to marry and to found a family. They are entitled to equal rights as to marriage, during marriage and at its dissolution.

"(2) Marriage shall be entered into only with the free and full consent of the intending spouses."

Recalling further that the General Assembly of the United Nations declared, by resolution 843 (IX) of 17 December 1954, that certain customs, ancient laws and practices relating to marriage and the family were inconsistent with the principles set forth in the Charter of the United Nations and in the Universal Declaration of Human Rights,

Reaffirming that all States, including those which have or assume responsibility for the administration of Non-Self-

Governing and Trust Territories until their achievement of independence, should take all appropriate measures with a view to abolishing such customs, ancient laws and practices by ensuring, *inter alia,* complete freedom in the choice of a spouse, eliminating completely child marriages and the betrothal of young girls before the age of puberty, and establishing appropriate penalties where necessary and establishing a civil or other register in which all marriages will be recorded,

Hereby agree as hereinafter provided:

Article 1

1. No marriage shall be legally entered into without the full and free consent of both parties, such consent to be expressed by them in person after due publicity and in the presence of the authority competent to solemnize the marriage and of witnesses, as prescribed by law.

2. Notwithstanding anything in paragraph 1 above, it shall not be necessary for one of the parties to be present when the competent authority is satisfied that the circumstances are exceptional and that the party has, before a competent authority and in such manner as may be prescribed by law, expressed and not withdrawn consent.

Article 2

States parties to the present Convention shall take legislative action to specify a minimum age for marriage. No marriage shall be legally entered into by any person under this age, except where a competent authority has granted a dispensation as to age, for serious reasons, in the interest of the intending spouses.

Article 3

All marriages shall be registered in an appropriate official register by the competent authority.

Article 4

1. The present Convention shall, until 31 December 1963, be open for signature on behalf of all States Members of the United Nations or members of any of the specialized agencies, and of any other State invited by the General Assembly of the United Nations to become party to the Convention.

2. The present Convention is subject to ratification. The instruments of ratifications shall be deposited with the Secretary-General of the United Nations.

Article 5

1. The present Convention shall be open for accession to all States referred to in Article 4, paragraph 1.

2. Accession shall be effected by the deposit of an instrument of accession with the Secretary-General of the United Nations.

Article 6

1. The present Convention shall come into force on the ninetieth day following the date of deposit of the eighth instrument of ratification or accession.

2. For each State ratifying or acceding to the Convention after the deposit of the eighth instrument of ratification or accession, the Convention shall enter into force on the ninetieth day after deposit by such State of its instrument of ratification or accession.

Article 7

1. Any Contracting State may denounce the present Convention by written notification to the Secretary-General of the United Nations. Denunciation shall take effect one year after the date of receipt of the notification by the Secretary-General.

2. The present Convention shall cease to be in force as from the date when the denunciation which reduces the number of parties to less than eight becomes effective.

Article 8

Any dispute which may arise between any two or more Contracting States concerning the interpretation or application of the present Convention which is not settled by negotiation shall, at the request of all the parties to the dispute, be referred to the International Court of Justice for decision, unless the parties agree to another mode of settlement.

Article 9

The Secretary-General of the United Nations shall notify all States Members of the United Nations and the non-member States contemplated in Article 4, paragraph 1, of the present Convention of the following:

(a) signatures and instruments of ratification received in accordance with Article 4;

(b) instruments of accession received in accordance with Article 5;

(c) the date upon which the Convention enters into force in accordance with Article 6;

(d) notification of denunciation received in accordance with Article 7, paragraph 1;

(e) abrogation in accordance with Article 7, paragraph 2.

Article 10

1. The present Convention, of which the Chinese, English, French, Russian and Spanish texts shall be equally authentic, shall be deposited in the archives of the United Nations.

2. The Secretary-General of the United Nations shall transmit a certified copy of the Convention to all States Members of the United Nations and to the non-member States contemplated in Article 4, paragraph 1.

In faith whereof the undersigned, being duly authorized, have signed on behalf of their respective Governments, the present Convention which was opened for signature at the Headquarters of the United Nations, New York, on the tenth day of December, one thousand nine hundred and sixty-two.

Recommenation on Consent to Marriage, Minimum Age for Marriage and Registration of Marriages

[General Assembly Resolution 2018 (XX) of 1 November 1965]

The General Assembly,

Recognizing that the family group should be strengthened because it is the basic unit of every society, and that men and women of full age have the right to marry and to found a family, that they are entitled to equal rights as to marriage and that marriage shall be entered into only with the free and full consent of the intending spouses, in accordance with the provisions of Article 16 of the Universal Declaration of Human Rights,

Recalling its resolution 843 (IX) of 17 December 1954,

Recalling further Article 2 of the Supplementary Convention on the Abolition of Slavery, the Slave Trade, and institutions and Practices Similar to Slavery of 1956, which makes certain provisions concerning the age of marriage, consent to marriage and registration of marriages,

Recalling also that Article 13, paragraph 1 b, of the Charter of the United Nations provides that the General Assembly shall make recommendations for the purpose of assisting in the realization of human rights and fundamental freedoms for all without distinction as to race, sex, language or religion,

Recalling likewise that, under Article 64 of the Charter, the Economic and Social Council may make arrangements with the Members of the United Nations to obtain reports on the steps taken to give effects to its own recommendations and to recommendations on matters falling within its competence made by the General Assembly,

1. Recommends, that, where not already provided by existing legislative or other measures, each Member State should take the necessary steps, in accordance with its constitutional processes, to adopt such legislative or other measures as may be appropriate to give effect to the following principles:

Principle I

(a) No marriage shall be legally entered into without the full and free consent of both parties, such consent to be expressed by them in person, after due publicity and in the presence of the authority competent to solemnize the marriage and of witnesses, as prescribed by law.

(b) Marriage by proxy shall be permitted only when the competent authorities are satisfied that each party has, before a competent authority and in such manner as may be prescribed by law, fully and freely expressed consent before witnesses and not withdrawn such consent.

Principle II

Member States shall take legislative action to specify a minimum age for marriage, which in any case shall not be less than fifteen years of age; no marriage shall be legally entered into by any person under this age, except where a competent authority has granted a dispensation as to age, for serious reasons, in the interest of the intending spouses.

Principle III

All marriages shall be registered in an appropriate official register by the competent authority.

2. Recommends that each Member State should bring the Recommendation on Consent to Marriage, Minimum Age for Marriage and Registration of Marriages contained in the present resolution before the authorities competent to enact legislation or to take other action at the earliest practicable moment and, if possible, no later than eighteen months after the adoption of the Recommendation;

3. Recommends that Member States should inform the Secretary-General, as soon as possible after the action referred to in paragraph 2 above, of the measures taken under the present Recommendation to bring it before the competent authority or authorities, with particulars regarding the authority or authorities considered as competent;

4. Recommends further that Member States should report to the Secretary-General at the end of three years, and thereafter at intervals of five years, on their law and practice with regard to the matters dealt with in the present Recommendation, showing the extent to which effect has been given or is proposed to be given to the provisions of the Recommendation and such modifications as have been found or may be found necessary in adapting or applying it;

5. Requests the Secretary-General to prepare for the Commission on the Status of Women a document containing the reports received from Governments concerning methods of implementing the three basic principles of the present Recommendation;

6. Invites the commission on the Status of Women to examine the reports received from Member States pursuant to the present Recommendation and to report thereon to the Economic and Social Council with such recommendations as it may deem fitting.

Declaration on the Protection of Women and Children in Emergency and Armed Conflict

[Resolution adopted by the General Assembly
14 December 1974—GAOR 29, Supp. 31, U.N. Doc. A/9631]

Editor's Comments. *In the evolution of the international political and intellectual order, few areas of tension have been as intense as that which has defined claims of "military necessity" and humanitarian law. War, a form of hostile relationship between or within (in case of the civil kind) states, is legal. And the core objective in engaging in such hostilities has always been the defeat of the enemy, with most action taken to effectuate that end generally regarded as "justified by military necessity." On the other hand, the idea that states have a right to defend themselves and pursue their self-defined interest by a variety of means including war has had to face an equally powerful view that nations have a duty, on humanitarian grounds, to observe prohibitions against violence not necessary for the achievement of war aims. In modern times, "military necessity" has had the ascendancy. But history and the human rights regime have changed matters, tilting them increasingly in favor of the humanitarian outlook.*

This history can best be understood through the principle of reciprocity, which means that one side to a conflict would observe certain restraints in its conduct providing the other side, in return, acted likewise. But during World Wars I and II, restraints were forgotten, as combatants and their political leaders seem to have lost their "public conscience" and sense of decency. The shock and disgust which resulted from the moral foulness of those wars sponsored moves toward a human rights emphasis as exampled by the Fourth Geneva Convention of 1949 which, among other things, forbids "outrages upon personal dignity," in particular "humiliating and degrading treatment,"[5] regardless of race, color, religion or sex. The main attribute of this convention is that it is not based on reciprocity; it is linked to humanity—all human beings, irrespective of their status as "enemies," should not, by virtue of their humanity, be subject to certain types of treatment.

Subsequent attempts to develop this area of international law pertaining to war include the United Nations and the International Committee of the Red Cross (ICRC). In the United Nations, two important documents bearing the identical title of "Report on Respect for Human Rights in Armed Conflicts"[6] were produced in 1969 and 1970, respectively. These documents admirably analyze many of the gaps in the existing law defining armed conflicts, including guerilla and internal warfare. The ICRC, on the other hand, organized two sessions (1971 and 1972) of a Conference of Government Experts in Geneva to draft additional rules to the 1949 Geneva Conventions on armed conflicts. The result has been two additional instruments called Protocol I, which deals with the Protection of Victims of International Armed Conflicts and Protocol II that concerns itself with the Protection of Victims of Non-International Armed Conflicts.[7]

It is within the context of all these efforts to ensure human rights during warfare that one must see the Declaration on the Protection of Women and Children in Emergency and Armed Conflict. Proclaimed on December 14, 1974, the Declaration takes note of mothers, "who play an important role in society, in the family and particularly the upbringing of children," and prohibits, for example, attacks and bombings on the civilian population, "especially on women and children, who are the most vulnerable members of the population."[8] The full text follows.

The General Assembly,

Having considered the recommendation of the Economic and Social Council contained in its resolution 1861 (LVI) of 16 May 1974,

Expressing its deep concern over the sufferings of women and children belonging to the civilian population who in periods of emergency and armed conflicts in the struggle for peace, self-determination, national liberation and independence are too often the vicims of inhuman acts and consequently suffer serious harm,

Aware of the suffering of women and children in many areas of the world, especially in those areas subject to suppression, aggression, colonialism, racism, alien domination and foreign subjugation,

Deeply concerned by the fact that, despite general and unequivocal condemnation, colonialism, racism and alien and foreign domination continue to subject many peoples under their yoke, cruelly suppressing the national liberation movements and inflicting heavy losses and incalculable sufferings on the populations under their domination, including women and children,

Deploring the fact that grave attacks are still being made on fundamental freedoms and the dignity of the human person and that colonial and racist foreign domination Powers continue to violate international humanitarian law,

Recalling the relevant provisions contained in the instruments of international humanitarian law relative to the protection of women and children in time of peace and war,

Recalling, among other important documents, its resolutions 2444 (XXIII) of 19 December 1968, 2597 (XXIV) of 16 December 1969 and 2674 (XXV) and 2675 (XXV) of 9 December 1970, on respect for human rights and on basic principles for the protection of civilian populations in armed conflicts, as well as Economic and Social Council resolution 1515 (XLVIII) of 29 May 1970 in which the Council requested the General Assembly to consider the possibility of drafting a declaration on the protection of women and children in emergency or wartime,

Conscious of its responsibility for the destiny of the rising generation and for the destiny of mothers, who play an important role in society, in the family and particularly in the upbringing of children,

Bearing in mind the need to provide special protection of women and children belonging to the civilian population,

Solemnly proclaims this Declaration on the Protection of Women and Children in Emergency and Armed Conflict and calls for the strict observance of the Declaration by all Member States:

1. Attacks and bombings on the civilian population, inflicting incalculable suffering, especially on women and children, who are the most vulnerable members of the population, shall be prohibited and such acts shall be condemned.

2. The use of chemical and bacteriological weapons in the course of military operations constitutes one of the most flagrant violations of the Geneva Protocol of 1925, the Geneva Conventions of 1949 and the principles of international humanitarian law and inflicts heavy losses on civilian populations, including defenceless women and children, and shall be severely condemned.

3. All States shall abide fully by their obligations under the Geneva Protocol of 1925 and the Geneva Conventions of 1949, as well as other instruments of international law relative to respect for human rights in armed conflicts, which offer important guarantees for the protection of women and children.

4. All efforts shall be made by States involved in armed conflicts, military operations in foreign territories or military operations in territories still under colonial domination to spare women and children from the ravages of war. All the necessary steps shall be taken to ensure the prohibition of measures such as persecution, torture, punitive measures, degrading treatment and violence, particularly against that part of the civilian population that consists of women and children.

5. All forms of repression and cruel and inhuman treatment of women and children, including imprisonment, torture, shooting, mass arrests, collective punishment, destruction of dwellings and forcible eviction, committed by belligerents in the course of military operations or in occupied territories shall be considered criminal.

6. Women and children belonging to the civilian population and finding themselves in circumstances of emergency and

armed conflict in the struggle for peace, self-determination, national liberation and independence, or who live in occupied territories, shall not be deprived of shelter, food, medical aid or other inalienable rights, in accordance with the provisions of the Universal Declaration of Human Rights, the International Covenant on Civil and Political Rights, the International Covenant on Economic, Social and Cultural Rights, the Declaration of the Rights of the Child or other instruments of international law.

Convention (No. 156) Concerning Equal Opportunities and Equal Treatment for Men and Women Workers: Workers with Family Responsibilities

Editor's Comments. *There are those who would have included this convention under the section of the book that deals with employment. The view of this writer, however, is that its unique attribute is that it is the only ILO convention (one may say the only international convention) that expressly covers distinctions made on the basis of* family *responsibilities. As such, it properly belongs in this section.*

Previously covered in this work are treaties such as the Equal Remuneration Convention and the Discrimination (Employment and Occupation) Convention[9] — each seeking to outlaw discrimination based on sex. In every case, however, there seemed to have been the subtle implication that family responsibilities are primarily a woman's concern. Even the 1979 Convention on the Elimination of All Forms of Discrimination Against Women — without doubt the most important treaty to date dealing with women's rights — went only so far as to assert that "a change in the traditional role of men as well as the role of women in society and in the family *is needed to achieve full equality between men and women. [Emphasis added.]"[10]*

Adopted by the ILO on June 23, 1981, the Workers with Family Responsibilities Convention takes the position that the care and upbringing of children is the shared responsibility of men and women as well as society as a whole. *When stated in such a manner, one finds not only an acknowledgement of the benefits society enjoys from the rearing of children but the age-old debt due to women for the uncompensated (and frequently unrecognized) burden they have borne in having to assume the primary responsibility for child rearing. It does more; it makes all the more urgent the call for national policies to implement the terms of the convention — especially as it seeks to confer on women a real equal opportunity to pursue their material well-being and their spiritual development.*

The convention "applies to men and women workers with

responsibilities in relation to dependent children" as well as "to other members of their immediate family who clearly need their care and support."[11] It requires states to take "all measures compatible with national conditions"[12] for the development of community services such as child care and family service facilities and for vocational training that will enable workers with family responsibilities "to become and remain integrated in the work force."[13] It also provides that "family responsibilities shall not, as such, constitute a valid reason for termination of employment."[14]

On the very day the convention was adopted, the ILO also accepted the Workers with Family Responsibilities Recommendation. Included in this section, the recommendation gives certain detailed suggestions to facilitate the implementation of the convention. The full text follows.

The General Conference of the International Labour Organisation,

Having been convened at Geneva by the Governing Body of the International Labour Office and having met in its Sixty-seventh Session on 3 June 1981, and

Noting the Declaration of Philadelphia concerning the Aims and Purposes of the International Labour Organisation which recognises that "all human beings, irrespective of race, creed or sex, have the right to pursue their material well-being and their spiritual development in conditions of freedom and dignity, of economic security and equal opportunity" and

Noting the terms of the Declaration on Equality of Opportunity and Treatment for Women Workers and of the resolution concerning a plan of action with a view to promoting equality of opportunity and treatment for women workers, adopted by the International Labour Conference in 1975, and

Noting the provisions of international labour Conventions and Recommendations aimed at ensuring equality of opportunity and treatment for men and women workers, namely the Equal Remuneration Convention and Recommendation, 1951, the Discrimination (Employment and Occupation) Convention and Recommendation, 1958, and Part VIII of the Human Resources Development Recommendation, 1975, and

Recalling that the Discrimination (Employment and Occupation) Convention, 1958, does not expressly cover distinctions made on the basis of family responsibilities, and considering that supplementary standards are necessary in this respect, and

Noting the terms of the Employment (Women with Family Reponsibilities) Recommendation, 1965, and considering the changes which have taken place since its adoption, and

Noting that instruments on equality of opportunity and treatment for men and women have also been adopted by the United Nations and other specialised agencies, and recalling, in particular, the fourteenth paragraph of the Preamble of the United Nations Convention on the Elimination of All Forms of Discrimination against Women, 1979, to the effect that States Parties are "aware that a change in the traditional role of men as well as the role of women in society and in the family is needed to achieve full equality between men and women," and

Recognising that the problems of workers with family responsibilities are aspects of wider issues regarding the family and society which should be taken into account in national policies, and

Recognising the need to create effective equality of opportunity and treatment as between men and women workers with family responsibilities and between such workers and other workers, and

Considering that many of the problems facing all workers are aggravated in the case of workers with family responsibilities and recognising the need to improve the conditions of the latter both by measures responding to their special needs and by measures designed to improve the conditions of workers in general, and

Having decided upon the adoption of certain proposals with regard to equal opportunities and equal treatment for men and women workers: workers with family responsibilities, which is the fifth item on the agenda of the session, and

Having determined that these proposals shall take the form of an international Convention,

adopts this twenty-third day of June of the year one thousand nine hundred and eighty-one the following Convention, which may be cited as the Workers with Family Responsibilities Convention, 1981:

Article 1

1. This Convention applies to men and women workers with responsibilities in relation to their dependent children, where such responsibilities restrict their possibilities of preparing for, entering, participating in or advancing in economic activity.

2. The provisions of this Convention shall also be applied to men and women workers with responsibilities in relation to other members of their immediate family who clearly need their care or support, where such responsibilities restrict their possibilities of preparing for, entering, participating in or advancing in economic activity.

3. For the purposes of this Convention, the terms "dependent child" and other member of the immediate family who clearly needs care or support" mean persons defined as such in each country by one of the means referred to in Article 9 of this Convention.

4. The workers covered by virtue of paragraphs 1 and 2 of this Article are hereinafter referred to as "workers with family responsibilities."

Article 2

This Convention applies to all branches of economic activity and all categories of workers.

Article 3

1. With a view to creating effective equality of opportunity and treatment for men and women workers, each Member shall make it an aim of national policy to enable persons with family responsibilities who are engaged or wish to engage in employment to exercise their right to do so without being subject to discrimination and, to the extent possible, without conflict between their employment and family responsibilities.

2. For the purposes of paragraph 1 of this Article, the term "discrimination" means discrimination in employment and occupation as defined by Articles 1 and 5 of the Discrimination (Employment and Occupation) Convention, 1958.

Article 4

With a view to creating effective equality of opportunity and treatment for men and women workers, all measures compatible with national conditions and possibilities shall be taken —

(a) to enable workers with family responsibilities to exercise their right to free choice of employment; and

(b) to take account of their needs in terms and conditions of employment and in social security.

Article 5

All measures compatible with national conditions and possibilities shall further be taken —

(a) to take account of the needs of workers with family responsibilities in community planning; and

(b) to develop or promote community services, public or private, such as childcare and family services and facilities.

Article 6

The competent authorities and bodies in each country shall take appropriate measures to promote information and education which engender broader public understanding of the principle of equality of opportunity and treatment for men and women workers and of the problems of workers with family responsibilities, as well as a climate of opinion conducive to overcoming these problems.

Article 7

All measures compatible with national conditions and possibilities, including measures in the field of vocational guidance and training, shall be taken to enable workers with family responsibilities to become and remain integrated in the labour force, as well as to re-enter the labour force after an absence due to those responsibilities.

Article 8

Family responsibilities shall not, as such, constitute a valid reason for termination of employment.

Article 9

The provisions of this Convention may be applied by laws or regulations, collective agreements, work rules, arbitration awards, court decisions or a combination of these methods, or in any other manner consistent with national practice which may be appropriate, account being taken of national conditions.

Article 10

1. The provisions of this Convention may be applied by stages if necessary, account being taken of national conditions: Provided that such measures of implementation as are taken shall apply in any case to all the workers covered by Article 1, paragraph 1.

2. Each Member which ratifies this Convention shall indicate in the first report on the application of the Convention

submitted under Article 22 of the Constitution of the International Labour Organisation in what respect, if any, it intends to make use of the faculty given by paragraph 1 of this Article, and shall state in subsequent reports the extent to which effect has been given or is proposed to be given to the Convention in that respect.

Article 11

Employers' and workers' organisations shall have the right to participate, in a manner appropriate to national conditions and practice, in devising and applying measures designed to give effect to the provisions of this Convention.

Article 12

The formal ratifications of this Convention shall be communicated to the Director-General of the International Labour Office for registration.

Article 13

1. This Convention shall be binding only upon those Members of the International Labour Organisation whose ratifications have been registered with the Director-General.

2. It shall come into force twelve months after the date on which the ratifications of two Members have been registered with the Director-General.

3. Thereafter, this Convention shall come into force for any Member twelve months after the date on which its ratification has been registered.

Article 14

1. A Member which has ratified this Convention may denounce it after the expiration of ten years from the date on which the Convention first comes into force, by an act communicated to the Director-General of the International Labour Office for registration. Such denunciation shall not take effect until one year after the date on which it is registered.

2. Each Member which has ratified this Convention and which does not, within the year following the expiration of the period of ten years mentioned in the preceding paragraph, exercise the right of denunciation provided for in this Article, will be bound for another period of ten years and, there-after, may denounce this Convention at the expiration of each period of ten years under the terms provided for in this Article.

Article 15

1. The Director-General of the International Labour Office shall notify all Members of the International Labour Organisation of the registration of all ratifications and denun-ciations communicated to him by the Members of the Organi-sation.

2. When notifying the Members of the Organisation of the registration of the second ratification communicated to him, the Director-General shall draw the attention of the Members of the Organisation to the date upon which the Convention will come into force.

Article 16

The Director-General of the International Labour Office shall communicate the the Secretary-General of the United Nations for registration in accordance with Article 102 of the Charter of the United Nations full particulars of all ratifications and acts of denunciation registered by him in accordance with the provisions of the preceding Articles.

Article 17

At such times as it may consider necessary, the Governing Body of the International Labour Office shall present to the General Conference a report on the working of this Conven-tion and shall examine the desirability of placing on the agenda of the Conference the question of its revision in whole or in part.

Article 18

1. Should the Conference adopt a new Convention revising this Convention in whole or in part, then, unless the new Convention otherwise provides—

(a) the ratification by a Member of the new revising Convention shall *ipso jure* involve the immediate denunciation of this Convention, notwithstanding the provisions of Article 14 above, if and when the new revising Convention shall have come into force;

(b) as from the date when the new revising Convention comes into force this convention shall cease to be open to ratification by the Members.

2. This Convention shall in any case remain in force in its actual form and content for those Members which have ratified it but have not ratified the revising Convention.

Article 19

The English and French versions of the text of this Convention are equally authoritative.

Recommendation (No. 165) Concerning Equal Opportunities and Equal Treatment for Men and Women Workers: Workers with Family Responsibilities

The General Conference of the International Labour Organisation,

Having been convened at Geneva by the Governing Body of the International Labour Office and having met in its Sixty-seventh Session on 3 June 1981, and

Noting the Declaration of Philadelphia concerning the Aims and Purposes of the International Labour Organisation which recognises that "all human beings, irrespective of race, creed or sex, have the right to pursue their material well-being and their spiritual development in conditions of freedom and dignity, of economic security and equal opportunity," and

Noting the terms of the Declaration on Equality of Opportunity and Treatment for Women Workers and of the resolution concerning a plan of action with a view to promoting equality of opportunity and treatment for women workers, adopted by the International Labour Conference in 1975, and

Noting the provisions of international labour Conventions and Recommendations aimed at ensuring equality of opportunity and treatment for men and women workers, namely the Equal Remuneration Convention and Recommendation, 1951, the Discrimination (Employment and Occupation) Convention and Recommendation, 1958, and Part VIII of the Human Resources Development Recommendation, 1975, and

Recalling that the Discrimination (Employment and Occupation) Convention, 1958, does not expressly cover distinctions made on the basis of family responsibilities, and considering that supplementary standards are necessary in this respect, and

Noting the terms of the Employment (Women with Family Responsibilities) Recommendation, 1965, and considering the changes which have taken place since its adoption, and

Noting that instruments on equality of opportunity and treatment for men and women have also been adopted by the United Nations and other specialised agencies, and recalling, in particular, the fourteenth paragraph of the Preamble of the United Nations Convention on the Elimination of All Forms of Discrimination Against Women, 1979, to the effect that States Parties are "aware that a change in the traditional role of men as well as the role of women in society and in the family is needed to achieve full equality between men and women," and

Recognising that the problems of workers with family responsibilities are aspects of wider issues regarding the family and society which should be taken into account in national policies, and

Recognising the need to create effective equality of opportunity and treatment as between men and women workers with family responsibilities and between such workers and other workers, and

Considering that many of the problems facing all workers are aggravated in the case of workers with family responsibilities, and recognising the need to improve the conditions of the latter both by measures responding to their special needs and by measures designed to improve the conditions of workers in general, and

Having decided upon the adoption of certain proposals with regard to equal opportunities and equal treatment for men and women workers: workers with family responsibilities, which is the fifth item on the agenda of the session, and

Having determined that these proposals shall take the form of a Recommendation, adopts this twenty-third day of June of the year one thousand nine hundred and eighty-one the following Recommendation, which may be cited as the Workers with Family Responsibilities Recommendation, 1981:

I. Definition, Scope and Means of Implementation

1. (1) This Recommendation applies to men and women workers with responsibilities in relation to their dependent children, where such responsibilities restrict their possibilities of preparing for, entering, participating in or advancing in economic activity.

(2) The provisions of this Recommendation should also be applied to men and women workers with responsibilities in relation to other members of their immediate family who need their care or support, where such responsibilities restrict their possibilities of preparing for, entering, participating in or advancing in economic activity.

(3) For the purposes of this Recommendation, the terms "dependent child" and "other member of the immediate family who needs care or support" mean persons defined as such in each country by one of the means referred to in paragraph 3 of this Recommendation.

(4) The workers covered by virtue of subparagraphs (1) and (2) of this paragraph are hereinafter referred to as "workers with family responsibilities."

2. This Recommendation applies to all branches of economic activity and all categories of workers.

3. The provisions of this Recomendation may be applied by laws or regulations, collective agreements, works rules, arbitration awards, court decisions or a combination of these methods, or in any other manner consistent with national practice which may be appropriate, account being taken of national conditions.

4. The provisions of this Recommendation may be applied by stages if necessary, account being taken of national

conditions: Provided that such measures of implementation as are taken should apply in any case to all the workers covered by paragraph 1, subparagraph (1).

5. Employers' and workers' organisations should have the right to participate, in a manner appropriate to national conditions and practice, in devising and applying measures designed to give effect to the provisions of this Recommendation.

II. National Policy

6. With a view to creating effective equality of opportunity and treatment for men and women workers, each Member should make it an aim of national policy to enable persons with family responsibilities who are engaged or wish to engage in employment to exercise their right to do so without being subject to discrimination and, to the extent possible, without conflict between their employment and family responsibilities.

7. Within the framework of a national policy to promote equality of opportunity and treatment for men and women workers, measures should be adopted and applied with a view to preventing direct or indirect discrimination on the basis of marital status or family responsibilities.

8. (1) For the purposes of paragraphs 6 and 7 above, the term "discrimination" means discrimination in employment and occupation as defined by Article 1 and 5 of the Discrimination (Employment and Occupation) Convention, 1958.

(2) During a transitional period special measures aimed at achieving effective equality between men and women workers should not be regarded as discriminatory.

9. With a view to creating effective equality of opportunity and treatment for men and women workers, all measures compatible with national conditions and possibilities should be taken—

(a) to enable workers with family responsibilities to exercise their right to vocational training and to free choice of employment;

(b) to take account of their needs in terms and conditions of employment and in social security; and

(c) to develop or promote child-care, family and other community services, public or private, responding to their needs.

10. The competent authorities and bodies in each country should take appropriate measures to promote information and education which engender broader public understanding of the principle of equality of opportunity and treatment for men and women workers and of the problems of workers with family responsibilities, as well as a climate of opinion conducive to overcoming these problems

11. The competent authorities and bodies in each country should take appropriate measures—

(a) to undertake or promote such research as may be necessary into the various aspects of the employment of workers with family responsibilities with a view to providing objective information on which sound policies and measures may be based; and

(b) to promote such education as will encourage the sharing of family responsibilities between men and women and enable workers with family responsibilities better to meet their employment and family responsibilities.

III. Training and Employment

12. All measures compatible with national conditions and possibilities should be taken to enable workers with family responsibilities to become and remain integrated in the labour force, as well as to re-enter the labour force after an absence due to those responsibilities.

13. In accordance with national policy and practice, vocational training facilities and, where possible, paid educational leave arrangements to use such facilities should be made available to workers with family responsibilities.

14. Such services as may be necessary to enable workers with

family responsibilities to enter or re-enter employment should be available, within the framework of existing services for all workers or, in default thereof, along lines appropriate to national conditions; they should include, free of charge to the workers, vocational guidance, counselling, information and placement services which are staffed by suitably trained personnel and are able to respond adequately to the special needs of workers with family responsibilities.

15. Workers with family responsibilities should enjoy equality of opportunity and treatment with other workers in relation to preparation for employment, access to employment, advancement within employment and employment security.

16. Marital status, family situation or family responsbilities should not, as such, constitute valid reasons for refusal or termination of employment.

IV. Terms and Conditions of Employment

17. All measures compatible with national conditions and possibilities and with the legitimate interests of other workers should be taken to ensure that terms and conditions of employment are such as to enable workers with family responsibilities to reconcile their employment and family responsibilities.

18. Particular attention should be given to general measures for improving working conditions and the quality of working life, including measures aiming at—

(a) the progressive reduction of daily hours of work and the reduction of overtime, and

(b) more flexible arrangements as regards working schedules, rest periods and holidays,

account being taken of the stage of development and the particular needs of the country and of different sectors of activity.

19. Whenever practicable and appropriate, the special needs of workers, including those arising from family responsibilities, should be taken into account in shift-work arrangements and assignments to night work.

20. Family responsibilities and considerations such as the place of employment of the spouse and the possibilities of educating children should be taken into account when tranferring workers from one locality to another.

21. (1) With a view to protecting part-time workers, temporary workers and homeworkers, many of whom have family responsibilities, the terms and conditions on which these types of employment are performed should be adequately regulated and supervised.

(2) The terms and conditions of employment, including social security coverage, of part-time workers and temorary workers should be, to the extent possible, equivalent to those of full-time and permanent workers respectively; in appropriate cases, their entitlement may be calculated on a pro rata basis.

(3) Part-time workers should be given the option to obtain or return to full-time employment when a vacancy exists and when the circumstances which determined assignment to part-time employment no longer exist.

22. (1) Either parent should have the possibility, within a period immediately following maternity leave, of obtaining leave of absence (parental leave), without relinquishing employment and with rights resulting from employment being safeguarded.

(2) The length of the period following maternity leave and the duration and conditions of the leave of absence referred to in subparagraph (1) of this paragraph should be determined in each country by one of the means referred to in paragraph 3 of this Recommendation.

(3) The leave of absence referred to in subparagraph (1) of this paragraph may be introduced gradually.

23. (1) It should be possible for a worker, man or woman, with family responsibilities in relation to a dependent child to obtain leave of absence in the case of its illness.

(2) It should be possible for a worker with family responsibilities to obtain leave of absence in the case of the

illness of another member of the worker's immediate family who needs that worker's care or support.

(3) The duration and conditions of the leave of absence referred to in subparagraphs (1) and (2) of this paragraph should be determined in each country by one of the means referred to in paragraph 3 of this Recommmednation.

V. Child-care and Family Services and Facilities

24. With a view to determining the scope and character of the child-care and family services and facilities needed to assist workers with family responsibilities to meet their employment and family responsibilities, the competent authorities should, in co-operation with the public and private organisations concerned, in particular employers' and workers' organisations, and within the scope of their resources for collecting information, take such measures as may be necessary and appropriate—

(a) to collect and publish adequate statistics on the number of workers with family responsibilities engaged in or seeking employment and on the number and age of their children and of other dependents requiring care; and

(b) to ascertain, through systematic surveys conducted more particularly in local communities, the needs and preferences for child-care and family services and facilities.

25. The competent authorities should, in co-operation with the public and private organisations concerned, take appropriate steps to ensure that child-care and family services and facilities meet the needs and preferences so revealed; to this end they should, taking account of national and local circumstances and possibilities, in particular—

(a) encourage and facilitate the establishment, particularly in local communities, of plans for the systematic development of child-care and family services and facilities, and

(b) themselves organise or encourage and facilitate the provision of adequate and appropriate child-care and family services and facilities, free of charge or at a reasonable charge in accordance with the workers' ability to pay,

developed along flexible lines and meeting the needs of children of different ages, of other dependants requiring care and of workers with family responsibilities.

26. (1) Child-care and family services and facilities of all types should comply with standards laid down and supervised by the competent authorities.

(2) Such standards should prescribe in particular the equipment and hygienic and technical requirements of the services and facilities provided and the number and qualifications of the staff.

(3) The competent authorities should provide or help to ensure the provision of adequate training at various levels for the personnel needed to staff child-care and family services and facilities.

VI. *Social Security*

27. Social security benefits, tax-relief, or other appropriate measures consistent with national policy should, when necessary, be available to workers with family responsibilities.

28. During the leave of absence referred to in paragraphs 22 and 23, the workers concerned may, in conformity with national conditions and practice, and by one of the means referred to in paragraph 3 of this Recommendation, be protected by social security.

29. A worker should not be excluded from social security coverage by reference to the occupational activity of his or her spouse and entitlement to benefits arising from that activity.

30. (1) The family responsibilities of a worker should be an element to be taken into account in determining whether employment offered is suitable in the sense that refusal of the offer may lead to loss or suspension of unemployment benefits.

(2) In particular, where the employment offered involves moving to another locality, the consideration to be taken into account should include the place of employment of the spouse and the possibilities of educating children.

31. In applying paragraphs 27 to 30 of this Recommendation, a Member whose economy is insufficiently developed may take account of the national resources and social security arrangements available.

VII. Help in Exercise of Family Responsibilities

32. The competent authorities and bodies in each country should promote such public and private action as is possible to lighten the burden deriving from the family responsibilities of workers.

33. All measures compatible with national conditions and possibilities should be taken to develop home-help and home-care services which are adequately regulated and supervised and which can provide workers with family responsibilities, as necessary, with qualified assistance at a reasonable charge in accordance with their ability to pay.

34. Since many measures designed to improve the conditions of workers in general can have a favourable impact on those of workers with family responsibilities, the competent authorities and bodies in each country should promote such public and private action as is possible to make the provision of services in the community, such as public transport, supply of water and energy in or near workers' housing and housing with labour-saving layout, responsive to the needs of workers.

VIII. Effect on Existing Recommendations

35. This Recommendation supersedes the Employment (Women with Family Responsibilities) Recommendation, 1965.

V. Prostitution and Slavery

Today the exploitation of women and girls through prostitution and slavery is nothing short of an international scandal. Many governments which maintain military bases abroad, some governments which earn considerable amounts of foreign exchange from tourism, and business persons seeking "periods of relaxation and fun" are part of the problem. Knowingly or unwittingly, they engage in a sort of cooperation, if not complicity, with recruiters and pimps, owners of houses of prostitution, "massage parlors," "Turkish bath," and "saunas" in reducing women to what can amount to slavery. In some instances, tourists accept invitations to take, or to otherwise participate in, "sex tours," perhaps not knowing that the woman who furnished them with sex may have been coerced into doing so, found herself in circumstances in which she is powerless or in a situation where a failed attempt at escaping can promise death.

Many of the grim details surrounding sexual slavery and the forced prostitution of women can be found in Kathleen Barry's *Female Sexual Slavery* (New York, Avon, 1979) and a report delivered to the U.N. Economic and Social Council on March 17, 1983. The report, commissioned by the Secretary General of the United Nations to "make a synthesis of the surveys and studies on the traffic in persons and the exploitation of the prostitution of others," states:

> A review of the various collective (remote) and individual (immediate) cause of prostitution—poverty, emotional deprivation,

trickery and coercion on the part of procurers—makes it unnecessary to invoke any kind of mental weakness or supposed vicious inclination to explain why women fall into prostitution.

Once embarked on that course, they enter a stage of servitude. Denied any independence, forced in order to engage in their new activity, to abide by rules imposed by the "old hands," exposed to pressures, untempered by any competing influence . . . subjected by the procurer to a very effective discipline which metes out punishment with an (infrequent) admixture of reward, they immediately find themselves in a marginal situation and undergo psychological conditioning such as may be experienced by someone living in a community within a sect.[1]

Convention for the Suppression of the Traffic in Persons and of the Exploitation of the Prostitution of Others

[Vol. 96 U.N.T.S., p. 271]

Editor's Comments. *Supplanting a number of earlier treaties mentioned in its preamble on the subject of its concern, the Convention for the Suppression of the Traffic in Persons and of the Exploitation of the Prostitution of Others was adopted on December 2, 1949, and it entered into force on July 25, 1951. States that accept its terms assume the obligation to punish any person who procures, entices, or leads away another person for purposes of prostitution, or exploits the prostitution of another person, even if that person consents.[2] States also assume the duty to punish any person who keeps, manages, or knowingly finances or takes part in financing a brothel, or rents premises or part thereof for purposes of prostitution. And one who acts on preparation for, or accepts the commission of, any of the criminal conducts mentioned above is also to be punished.[3] In addition, the treaty includes provisions for extradition, exchange of victims of prostitution, temporary care, and repatriation.[4]*

Given the preceding examples of the convention's terms, one might assume that considerable progress is being made in limiting the traffic in persons and the exploitation of the prostitution of others. But, as should be perceived from the introduction to this section, such is not the case. Governments, in many instances, have failed to ratify the convention. Most of those which have ratified it, have been less than circumspect in enforcing its provisions.

The need to pressure states into ratifying the convention and supporting its implementation cannot be more urgent. The same should be done in respect of the Supplementary Convention on the Abolition of Slavery, the Slave Trade, and Institutions and Practices Similar to Slavery, which is included here because some of its provisions are increasingly being thought to be applicable to the conditions of women caught in the "trap of prostitution."

The Supplementary Convention on the Abolition of Slavery, the Slave Trade and Institutions and Practices Similar to Slavery came into force on April 30, 1957. The full text follows.

Preamble

Whereas prostitution and the accompanying evil of the traffic in persons for the purpose of prostitution are incompatible with the dignity and worth of the human person and endanger the welfare of the individual, the family and the community,

Whereas, with respect to the suppression of the traffic in women and children, the following international instruments are in force:

1. International Agreement of 18 May 1904 for the Suppression of the White Slave Traffic, as amended by the Protocol approved by the General Assembly of the United Nations on 3 December 1948,

2. International Convention of 4 May 1910 for the Suppression of the White Slave Traffic, as amended by the above-mentioned Protocol,

3. International Convention of 30 September 1921 for the Suppression of the Traffic in Women and Children, as amended by the Protocol approved by the General Assembly of the United Nations on 20 October 1947,

4. International Convention of 11 October 1933 for the Suppression of the Traffic in Women of Full Age, as amended by the aforesaid Protocol,

Whereas the League of Nations in 1937 prepared a draft Convention extending the scope of the above-mentioned instruments, and

Whereas developments since 1937 make feasible the conclusion of a convention consolidating the above-mentioned instruments and embodying the substance of the 1937 draft Convention as well as desirable alterations therein;

Now therefore

The Contracting Parties

Hereby agree as hereinafter provided:

Article 1

The Parties to the present Convention agree to punish any person who, to gratify the passions of another:

1. Procures, entices or leads away, for purposes of prostitution, another person, even with the consent of that person;

2. Exploits the prostitution of another person, even with the consent of that person.

Article 2

The Parties to the present Convention further agree to punish any person who:

1. Keeps or manages, or knowingly finances or takes part in the financing of a brothel;

2. Knowingly lets or rents a building or other place or any part thereof for the purpose of the prostituton of others.

Article 3

To the extent permitted by domestic law, attempts to commit any of the offences referred to in Articles 1 and 2, and acts preparatory to the commission thereof, shall also be punished.

Article 4

To the extent permitted by domestic law, intentional participation in the acts referred to in Articles 1 and 2 above shall also be punishable.

To the extent permitted by domestic law, acts of participation shall be treated as separate offences whenever this is necessary to prevent impunity.

Article 5

In cases where injured persons are entitled under domestic law to be parties to preceedings in respect of any of the offences referred to in the present Convention, aliens shall be so entitled upon the same terms as nationals.

Article 6

Each Party to the present Convention agrees to take all the necessary measures to repeal or abolish any existing law, regulation or administrative provision by virtue of which persons who engage in or are suspected of engaging in prostitution are subject either to special registration or the the possession of a special document or to any exceptional requirements for supervision or notification.

Article 7

Previous convictions pronounced in foreign States for offences referred to in the present Convention shall, to the extent permitted by domestic law, be taken into account for the purpose of:

1. Establishing recidivism;

2. Disqualifying the offender from the exercise of civil rights.

Article 8

The offences referred to in Articles 1 and 2 of the present Convention shall be regarded as extraditable offenses in any extradition treaty which has been or may hereafter be concluded between any of the Parties to this Convention.

The Parties to the present Convention which do not make extradition conditional on the existence of a treaty shall henceforward recognize the offences referred to in Articles 1 and 2 of the present Convention as cases for extradition between themselves.

Extradition shall be granted in accordance with the law of the State to which the request is made.

Article 9

In States where the extradition of nationals is not permitted by law, nationals who have returned to their own State after the commission abroad of any of the offences referred to in Articles 1 and 2 of the present Convention shall be prosecuted in and punished by the courts of their own State.

This provision shall not apply if, in a similar case between the Parties to the present Convention, the extradition of an alien cannot be granted.

Article 10

The provisions of Article 9 shall not apply when the person charged with the offence has been tried in a foreign State and, if convicted, has served his sentence or had it remitted or reduced in conformity with the laws of that foreign State.

Article 11

Nothing in the present Convention shall be interpreted as determining the attitude of a Party towards the general question of the limits of criminal jurisdiction under international law.

Article 12

The present Convention does not affect the principle that the offences to which it refers shall in each State be defined, prosecuted and punished in conformity with its domestic law.

Article 13

The Parties to the present Convention shall be bound to execute letters of request relating to offences referred to in the Convention in accordance with their domestic law and practice.

The transmission of letters of request shall be effected:

1. By direct communication between the judicial authorities; or

2. By direct communication between the Ministers of Justice of the two States, or by direct communication from

another competent authority of the State making the request to the Minister of Justice of the State to which the request is made; or

3. Through the diplomatic or consular representative of the State making the request in the State to which the request is made; this representative shall send the letters of request direct to the competent judicial authority or to the authority indicated by the Government of the State to which the request is made, and shall receive direct from such authority the papers constituting the execution of the letters of request.

In cases 1 and 3 a copy of the letters of request shall always be sent to the superior authority of the State to which application is made.

Unless otherwise agreed, the letters of request shall be drawn up in the language of the authority making the request, provided always that the State to which the request is made may require a translation in its own language, certified correct by the authority making the request.

Each Party to the present Convention shall notify to each of the other Parties to the Convention the method or methods of transmission mentioned above which it will recognize for the letters of request of the latter State.

Until such notification is made by a State, its existing procedure in regard to letters of request shall remain in force.

Execution of letters of request shall not give rise to a claim for reimbursement of charges or expenses of any nature whatever other than expenses of experts.

Nothing in the present Article shall be construed as an undertaking on the part of the Parties to the present Convention to adopt in criminal matters any form or methods of proof contrary to their own domestic laws.

Article 14

Each Party to the present Convention shall establish or maintain a service charged with the co-ordination and centralization of the results of the investigation of offences referred to in the present Convention.

Such services should compile all information calculated to facilitate the prevention and punishment of the offences referred to in the present Convention and should be in close contact with the corresponding services in other States.

Article 15

To the extent permitted by domestic law and to the extent to which the authorities responsible for the services referred to in Article 14 may judge desirable, they shall furnish to the authorities reponsible for the corresponding services in other States the following information:

1. Particulars of any offence referred to in the present convention or any attempt to commit such offence;

2. Particulars of any search for and any prosecution, arrest, conviction, refusal of admission or expulsion of persons guilty of any of the offences referred to in the present Convention, the movements of such persons and any other useful information with regard to them.

The information so furnished shall include descriptions of the offenders, their fingerprints, photographs, methods of operation, police records and records of conviction.

Article 16

The Parties to the present Convention agree to take or to encourage, through their public and private educational, health, social, economic and other related services, measures for the prevention of Prostitution and for the rehabilitation and social adjustment of the victims of prostitution and of the offences referred to in the present Convention.

Article 17

The Parties to the present Convention undertake, in connexion with immigration and emigration, to adopt or maintain such measures as are required in terms of their obligations under the present Convention, to check the traffic in persons of either sex for the purpose of prostitution.

In particular they undertake:

1. To make such regulations as are necessary for the protection of immigrants or emigrants, and in particular, women and children, both at the place of arrival and departure and while *en route;*

2. To arrange for appropriate publicity warning the public of the dangers of the aforesaid traffic;

3. To take appropriate measures to ensure supervision of railway stations, airports, seaports and *en route,* and of other public places, in order to prevent international traffic in persons for the purpose of prostitution;

4. To take appropriate measures in order that the appropriate authorities be informed of the arrival of persons who appear, *prima facie,* to be the principals and accomplices in or victims of such traffic.

Article 18

The Parties to the present Convention undertake, in accordance with the conditions laid down by domestic law, to have declarations taken from aliens who are prostitutes, in order to establish their identity and civil status and to discover who has caused them to leave their State. The information obtained shall be communicated to the authorities of the State of origin of the said persons with a view to their eventual repatriation.

Article 19

The Parties to the present Convention undertake, in accordance with the conditions laid down by domestic law and without prejudice to prosecution or other action for violations thereunder and so far as possible:

1. Pending the completion of arrangements for the repatriation of destitute victims of international traffic in persons for the purpose of prostitution, to make suitable provisions for their temporary care and maintenance;

2. To repatriate persons referred to in Article 18 who desire to be repatriated or who may be claimed by persons exercising

authority over them or whose explusion is ordered in conformity with the law. Repatriation shall take place only after agreement is reached with the State of destination as to identity and nationality as well as to the place and date of arrival at frontiers. Each Party to the present Convention shall facilitate the passage of such persons through its territory.

Where the persons referred to in the preceding paragraph cannot themselves repay the cost of repatriation and have neither spouse, relatives nor guardian to pay for them, the cost of repatriation as far as the nearest frontier or port of embarkation or airport in the direction of the State of origin shall be borne by the State where they are in residence, and the cost of the remainder of the journey shall be borne by the State of origin.

Article 20

The Parties to the present Convention shall, if they have not already done so, take the necessary measures for the supervision of employment agencies in order to prevent persons seeking employment, in particular women and children, from being exposed to the danger of prostitution.

Article 21

The Parties to the present Convention shall communicate to the Secretary-General of the United Nations such laws and regulations as have already been promulgated in their States, and thereafter annually such laws and regulations as may be promulgated, relating to the subjects of the present Conventions, as well as all measures taken by them concerning the application of the Convention. The information received shall be published periodically by the Secretary-General and sent to all Members of the United Nations and to non-member States to which the present Convention is officially communicated in accordance with Article 23.

Article 22

If any dispute shall arise between the Parties to the present Convention relating to its interpretation or application and if such dispute cannot be settled by other means, the dispute shall, at the request of any one of the Parties to the dispute, be referred to the International Court of Justice.

Article 23

The present Convention shall be open for signature on behalf of any Member of the United Nations and also on behalf of any other State to which an invitation has been addressed by the Economic and Social Council.

The present Convention shall be ratified and the instruments of ratification shall be deposited with the Secretary-General of the United Nations.

The States mentioned in the first paragraph which have not signed the Convention may accede to it.

Accession shall be effected by deposit of an instrument of accession with the Secretary-General of the United Nations.

For the purpose of the present Convention the word "State" shall include all the colonies and Trust Territories of a State signatory or acceding to the Convention and all territories for which such State is internationally responsible.

Article 24

The present Convention shall come into force on the ninetieth day following the date of deposit of the second instrument of ratification or accession.

For each State ratifying or acceding to the Convention after the deposit of the second instrument of ratification or accession, the Convention shall enter into force ninety days after the deposit by such State of its instrument of ratification or accession.

Article 25

After the expiration of five years from the entry into force of the present Convention, any Party to the Convention may denounce it by a written notification addressed to the Secretary-General of the United Nations.

Such denunciation shall take effect for the Party making it one year from the date upon which it is received by the Secretary-General of the United Nations.

Article 26

The Secretary-General of the United Nations shall inform all Members of the United Nations and non-member States referred to in Article 23:

(a) Of signatures, ratifications and accessions received in accordance with Article 23;

(b) Of the date on which the present Convention will come into force in accordance with Article 24;

(c) Of denunciations received in accordance with Article 25.

Article 27

Each Party to the present Convention undertakes to adopt, in accordance with its Constitution, the legislative or other measures necessary to ensure the application of the Convention.

Article 28

The provisions of the present Convention shall supersede in the relations between the Parties thereto the provisions of the international instruments referred to in sub-paragraphs 1, 2, 3, and 4 of the second paragraph of the Preamble, each of which shall be deemed to be terminated when all the Parties thereto shall have become parties to the present Convention.

In faith whereof the undersigned, being duly authorized thereto by their respective Governments, have signed the present Convention, opened for signature at Lake Success, New York, on the twenty-first day of March, one thousand nine hundred and fifty, a certified true copy of which shall be transmitted by the Secretary-General to all the Members of the United Nations and to the non-member States referred to in Article 23.

Supplementary Convention on the Abolition of Slavery, the Slave Trade, and Institutions and Practices Similar to Slavery

[Vol 266 U.N.T.S., p. 40]

Preamble

The States Parties to the present Convention

Considering that freedom is the birthright of every human being;

Mindful that the peoples of the United Nations reaffirmed in the Charter their faith in the dignity and worth of the human person;

Considering that the Universal Declaration of Human Rights, proclaimed by the General Assembly of the United Nations as a common standard of achievement for all peoples and all nations, states that no one shall be held in slavery or servitude and that slavery and the slave trade shall be prohibited in all their forms:

Recognizing that, since the conclusion of the Slavery Convention signed at Geneva on 25 September 1926, which was designed to secure the abolition of slavery and of the slave trade, further progress has been made towards this end;

Having regard to the Forced Labour Convention of 1930 and to subsequent action by the International Labour Organisation in regard to forced or compulsory labour;

Being aware, however, that slavery, the slave trade and institutions and practices similar to slavery have not yet been eliminated in all parts of the world;

Having decided, therefore, that the Convention of 1926, which remains operative, should now be augmented by the conclusion of a supplementary convention designed to intensify national as well as international efforts towards the abolition of slavery, the slave trade and institutions and practices similar to slavery;

Have agreed as follows:

Section I

INSTITUTIONS AND PRACTICES SIMILAR TO SLAVERY

Article 1

Each of the States Parties to this Convention shall take all practicable and necessary legislative and other measures to bring about progressively and as soon as possible the complete abolition or abandonment of the following institutions and practices, where they still exist and whether or not they are covered by the definition of slavery contained in Article 1 of the Slavery Convention signed at Geneva on 25 September 1926:

(a) Debt bondage, that is to say, the status or condition arising from a pledge by a debtor of his personal services or of those of a person under his control as security for a debt, if the value of those services as reasonably assessed is not applied towards the liquidation of the debt or the length and nature of those services are not respectively limited and defined;

(b) Serfdom, that is to say, the condition or status of a tenant who is by law, custom or agreement bound to live and labour on land belonging to another person and to render some determinate service to such other person, whether for reward or not, and is not free to change his status;

(c) Any institution or practice whereby:

   (i) A woman, without the right to refuse, is promised or given in marriage on payment of a consideration in money or in kind to her parents, guardian, family or any other person or group; or

   (ii) The husband of a woman, his family, or his clan, has the right to transfer her to another person for value received or otherwise; or

   (iii) A woman on the death of her husband is liable to be inherited by another person;

(d) Any institution or practice whereby a child or young person

under the age of 18 years is delivered by either or both of his natural parents or by his guardian to another person, whether for reward or not, with a view to the exploitation of the child or young person or of his labour.

Article 2

With a view to bringing to an end the institutions and practices mentioned in Article 1 *(c)* of this Convention, the States Parties undertake to prescribe, where appropriate, suitable minimum ages of marriage, to encourage the use of facilities whereby the consent of both parties to a marriage may be freely expressed in the presence of a competent civil or religious authority, and to encourage the registration of marriages.

SECTION II

THE SLAVE TRADE

Article 3

1. The act of conveying or attempting to convey slaves from one country to another by whatever means of transport, or of being accessory thereto, shall be a criminal offence under the laws of the States Parties to this Convention and persons convicted thereof shall be liable to very severe penalties.

2. *(a)* The States Parties shall take all effective measures to prevent ships and aircraft authorized to fly their flag from conveying slaves and to punish persons guilty of such acts or of using national flags for that purpose.

(b) The States Parties shall take all effective measures to ensure that their ports, airfields and coasts are not used for the conveyance of slaves.

3. The States Parties to this Convention shall exchange information in order to ensure the practical co-ordination of the measures taken by them in combating the slave trade and shall inform each other of every case of the slave trade, and of every

attempt to commit this criminal offence, which comes to their notice.

Article 4

Any slave who takes refuge on board any vessel of a State Party to this Convention shall *ipso facto* be free.

SECTION III

SLAVERY AND INSTITUTIONS AND PRACTICES SIMILAR TO SLAVERY

Article 5

In a country where the abolition or abandonment of slavery, or of the institutions or practices mentioned in Article 1 of this Convention, is not yet complete, the act of mutilating, branding or otherwise marking a slave or a person of servile status in order to indicate his status, or as a punishment, or for any other reason, or of being accessory thereto, shall be a criminal offence under the laws of the States Parties to this Convention and persons convicted thereof shall be liable to punishment.

Article 6

1. The act of enslaving another person or of inducing another person to give himself or a person dependent upon him into slavery, or of attempting these acts, or being accessory thereto, or being a party to a conspiracy to accomplish any such acts, shall be a criminal offence under the laws of the States Parties to this Convention and persons convicted thereof shall be liable to punishment.

2. Subject to the provisions of the introductory paragraph of Article 1 of this Convention, the provisions of paragraph 1 of the present Article shall also apply to the act of inducing another person to place himself or a person dependent upon him into the servile status resulting from any of the institutions or practices mentioned in Article 1, to any attempt to perform such acts, to bring accessory thereto, and to being a party to a conspiracy to accomplish any such acts.

SECTION IV

DEFINITIONS

Article 7

For the purposes of the present Convention:

(a) "Slavery" means, as defined in the Slavery Convention of 1926, the status or condition of a person over whom any or all of the powers attaching to the right of ownership are exercised, and "slave" means a person in such condition or status;

(b) "A person of servile status" means a person in the condition or status resulting from any of the institutions or practices mentioned in Article 1 of this Convention;

(c) "Slave trade" means and includes all acts involved in the capture, acquisition or disposal of a person with intent to reduce him to slavery; all acts involved in the acquisition of a slave with a view to selling or exchanging him; all acts of disposal by sale of exchange of a person acquired with a view to being sold or exchanged; and, in general, every act of trade or transport in slaves by whatever means of conveyance.

SECTION V

CO-OPERATION BETWEEN STATES PARTIES AND COMMUNICATION OF INFORMATION

Article 8

1. The States Parties to this Convention undertake to co-operate with each other and with the United Nations to give effect to the foregoing provisions.

2. The Parties undertake to communicate to the Secretary-General of the United Nations copies of any laws, regulations and administrative measures enacted or put into effect to implement the provisions of this Convention.

3. The Secretary-General shall communicate the information received under paragraph 2 of this Article to the other

Parties and to the Economic and Social Council as part of the documentation for any discussion which the Council might undertake with a view to making further recommendations for the abolition of slavery, the slave trade or the institutions and practices which are the subject of this Convention.

SECTION VI

FINAL CLAUSES

Article 9

No reservations may be made to this Convention.

Article 10

Any dispute between States Parties to this convention relating to its interpretation or application, which is not settled by negotiation, shall be referred to the International Court of Justice at the request of any one of the parties to the dispute, unless the parties concerned agree on another mode of settlement.

Article 11

1. This Convention shall be open until 1 July 1957 for signature by any State Member of the United Nations or of a specialized agency. It shall be subject to ratification by the signatory States, and the instruments of ratification shall be deposited with the Secretary-General of the United Nations, who shall inform each signatory and acceding State.

2. After 1 July 1957 this Convention shall be open for accession by any State Member of the United Nations or of a specialized agency, or by any other State to which an invitation to accede has been addressed by the General Assembly of the United Nations. Accession shall be effected by the deposit of a formal instrument with the Secretary-General of the United Nations, who shall inform each signatory and acceding State.

Article 12

1. This Convention shall apply to all nonself-governing, trust, colonial and other non-metropolitan territories for the international relations of which any State Party is responsible; the Party concerned shall, subject to the provisions of paragraph 2 of this Article, at the time of signature, ratification or accession declare the non-metropolitan territory or teritories to which the Convention shall apply *ipso facto* as a result of such signature, ratification or accession.

2. In any case in which the previous consent of a non-metropolitan territory is required by the constitutional laws or practices of the Party or of the non-metropolitan territory, the Party concerned shall endeavour to secure the needed consent of the non-metropolitan territory within the period of twelve months from the date of signature of the Convention by the metropolitan State, and when such consent has been obtained the Party shall notify the Secretary-General. This Convention shall apply to the territory or territories named in such notification from the date of its receipt by the Secretary-General.

3. After the expiry of the twelve-month period mentioned in the preceding paragraph, the States Parties concerned shall inform the Secretary-General of the results of the consultations with those non-metropolitan territories for whose international relations they are responsible and whose consent to the application of this Convention may have been withheld.

Article 13

1. This Convention shall enter into force on the date on which two States have become Parties thereto.

2. It shall thereafter enter into force with respect to each State and territory on the date of deposit of the instrument of ratification or accession of that State or notification of application to that territory.

Article 14

1. The application of this Convention shall be divided into

successive periods of three years, of which shall begin on the date of entry into force of the Convention in accordance with paragraph 1 of Article 13.

2. Any State Party may denounce this Convention by a notice addressed by that State to the Secretary-General not less than six months before the expiration of the current three-year period. The Secretary-General shall notify all other parties of each such notice and the date of the receipt thereof.

3. Denunciations shall take effect at the expiration of the current three-year period.

4. In cases where, in accordance with the provisions of Article 12, this Convention has become applicable to a non-metropolitan territory of a Party, that Party may at any time thereafter, with the consent of the territory concerned, give notice to the Secretary-General of the United Nations denouncing this Convention separately in respect of that territory. The denunciation shall take effect on the year after the date of the receipt of such notice by the Secretary-General, who shall notify all other Parties of such notice and the date of the receipt thereof.

Article 15

This Convention, of which the Chinese, English, French, Russian and Spanish texts are equally authentic, shall be deposited in the archives of the United Nations Secretariat. The Secretary-General shall prepare a certified copy thereof for communication to States Parties to this Convention, as well as to all other States Members of the United Nations and of the specialized agencies.

In witness whereof the undersigned, being duly authorized thereto by their respective Governments, have signed this Convention on the date appearing opposite their respective signatures.

Done at the European Office of the United Nations at Geneva, this seventh day of September one thousand nine hundred and fifty-six.

VI. Political Rights

For those who share the values of individual self-determination and political democracy, the right of individuals—including women—to vote in national and local elections now seems self-evident. Yet such was not always the case.

Up to World War II, women had the right to vote in national elections in relatively few countries. In the post–1945 period, however, a broad extension of the franchise has taken place with traditional holdouts such as Switzerland (1971), Portugal (1976), and Lichtenstein (1984) "joining the fold" of nation-states recognizing the right of women to vote. Today, only a few states such as Saudi Arabia and Kuwait still refuse to join that fold. The United Nations has been at the center of the "broad extension" mentioned above.

In one of its earliest decisions, the U.N. General Assembly, on December 11, 1946, recommended that all member states which had not granted women political rights equal to men should adopt the necessary measures to do so. And every year from 1948 to 1972, the Secretary-General prepared and circulated reports on the progress achieved in respect of the political rights of women. Those reports had important impacts, as states acted to have themselves presented in the most favorable light—as taking or having taken action to improve the political status of women. The most important step of the United Nations, however, was its adoption, in 1953, of the Convention on the Political Rights of Women.

That convention is not only about voting rights. It also

speaks to the broader spectrum of political rights. And as the discussions which preceded its adoption attest, considerable differences existed among members of the United Nations— differences which prevent women from enjoying many of the rights spelled out in the convention.[1] With stirring speeches during those discussions, states such as Lebanon expressed the sentiments of many which felt the time had come to right past wrongs. The history of humankind, it contended, is "replete with examples of unatonable mistakes and criminal madness . . . of all the crimes of man, however, the most shocking (has been) the unjust subjugation of women."[2] Others felt that while certain rights should be recognized, it was inadvisable to make women eligible "to hold public office" on equal terms with men, as provided by Article 3.

The most frequently identified concern during the debate was that of having women as officers in the military or as part of combat troops. That concern has just recently arisen in relationship to the January 1990 U.S. intervention in Panama, during which Captain Linda Bray served as Military Police Officer.[3] In the view of this writer, however, political leaders were and always have been equally or more concerned about having to reshape their respective countries into more truly democratic societies. Doing so would require the cooperative participation of women and men in *all* spheres of human activity. That type of society is the one that the Convention on the Political Rights of Women has sought, but it is also the kind that has eluded us.

While the right to vote and to hold public office is formally recognized, there is actually conspicuous under-representation of women at most levels of government, especially at the higher decision-making positions. In a 1985 world survey, although women constitute 52% of the enfranchised population in the United States, France and the United Kingdom, for example— countries that are perceived as democratic and enlightened— only 5% of their respective national legislature were women.[4]

Facts of the kind presented in the last sentence have urged the United Nations to remind states that women *must* be included in all senior and other professional positions in public life—not simply in health centers and institutions providing for the welfare of children or elderly persons—if their political rights are to be properly promoted. In view of these facts, the General Assembly in 1979 called upon governments "to take steps to ensure *effective* participation of women in the decision-making process with respect to foreign policy and international economic and political cooperation, including steps to ensure that they have equal access to diplomatic functions and that they are represented in the United Nations and other international organizations."[5] The 1985 World Conference to review and Appraise the Achievements of the U.N. Decade for Women was persuaded to demand that governments take action by the year 2000 to put into effect the terms of the convention.[6] The convention entered into force on July 7, 1954.

An Inter-American Convention on the Granting of Political Rights to Women was adopted by the nation-states of the Americas in 1948 and its text may be found in Appendix A. The Inter-American Convention does not deal explicitly with the right to "hold public office" or with the right to exercise "all public functions."

Convention on the Political Rights of Women

[Vol. 193 U.N.T.S., p. 135]

The Contracting Parties,

Desiring to implement the principle of equality of rights for men and women contained in the Charter of the United Nations,

Recognizing that everyone has the right to take part in the government of his country directly or through freely chosen representatives, and has the right to equal access to public service in his country, and desiring to equalize the status of men and women in the enjoyment and exercise of political rights, in accordance with the provisions of the Charter of the United Nations and of the Universal Declaration of Human Rights,

Having resolved to conclude a Convention for this purpose,

Hereby agree as hereinafter provided:

Article 1

Women shall be entitled to vote in all elections on equal terms with men, without any discrimination.

Article 2

Women shall be eligible for election to all publicly elected bodies, established by national law, on equal terms with men, without any discrimination.

Article 3

Women shall be entitled to hold public office and to exercise all public functions, established by national law, on equal terms with men, without any discrimination.

Article 4

1. This Convention shall be open for signature on behalf of

any other State to which an invitation has been addressed by the General Assembly.

2. This Convention shall be ratified and the instruments of ratification shall be deposited with the Secretary-General of the United Nations.

Article 5

1. This Convention shall be open for accession to all States referred to in paragraph 1 of Article 4.

2. Accession shall be effected by the deposit of an instrument of accession with the Secretary-General of the United Nations.

Article 6

1. This Convention shall come into force on the ninetieth day following the date of deposit of the sixth instrument of ratification of accession.

2. For each State ratifying or acceding to the Convention after the deposit of the sixth instrument of ratification or accession the Convention shall enter into force on the ninetieth day after deposit by such State of its instruments of ratification or accession.

Article 7

In the event that any State submits a reservation to any of the Articles of this Convention at the time of signature, ratification or accession, the Secretary-General shall communicate the text of the reservation to all States which are or may become parties to this Convention. Any State which objects to the reservation may, within a period of ninety days from the date of the said communication (or upon the date of its becoming a party to the Convention), notify the Secretary-General that it does not accept it. In such case, the Convention shall not enter into force as between such State and the State making the reservation.

Article 8

1. Any State may denounce this Convention by written notification to the Secretary-General of the United Nations. Denunciation shall take effect one year after the date of receipt of the notification by the Secretary-General.

2. This Convention shall cease to be in force as from the date when the denunciation which reduces the number of parties to less than six becomes effective.

Article 9

Any dispute which may arise between any two or more Contracting States concerning the interpretation or application of this Convention, which is not settled by negotiation, shall at the request of any one of the parties to the dispute be referred to the International Court of Justice for decision, unless they agree to another mode of settlement.

Article 10

The Secretary-General of the United Nations shall notify all Members of the United Nations and the non-member States contemplated in paragraph 1 of Article 4 of this Convention of the following:

(a) Signatures and instruments of ratifications received in accordance with Article 4;

(b) Instruments of accession received in accordance with Article 5;

(c) The date upon which this Convention enters into force in accordance with Article 6;

(d) Communications and notifications received in accordance with Article 7;

(e) Notifications of denunciation received in accordance with paragraph 1 of Article 8;

(f) Abrogation in accordance with paragraph 2 of Article 8.

Article 11

1. This Convention, of which the Chinese, English, French, Russian and Spanish texts shall be equally authentic, shall be deposited in the archives of the United Nations.

2. The Secretary-General of the United Nations shall transmit a certified copy to all Members of the United Nations and to the non-member States contemplated in paragraph 1 of Article 4.

VII. All Discrimination

The last section of this book includes what, using almost any standard of comparison with the preceding treaties, is the most important convention to date on the rights of women — the Convention on the Elimination of All Forms of Discrimination Against Women. It also includes the convention's intellectual ancestor — the 1967 Declaration on the Elimination of Discrimination Against Women. The section represents more, however; it focuses on the rights of women in the most gender-neutral manner.

Most of the other conventions are really corrective in character, in the sense that they identify women as a separate class of persons that requires special treatment. The goal of corrective treaties, such as the Convention Concerning Maternity Protection or the Convention Concerning the Nationality of Married Women, is to change and improve specific conduct, practices, or procedures toward women in some area, without making any overt comparison to the treatment of men in that area. In fact, they do not apply to men.

A few treaties, such as the Convention Concerning the Employment of Women in Underground Work in Mines of All Kinds[1] which provides that "no female, whatever her age, shall be employed in underground work in any mine,"[2] are protective. That is, they bespeak a societal view of women as a class of persons which either "should not or cannot engage in specific activities."[3] They imply that women are either subordinate or inferior to men. Finally, other treaties such as those in this section and the previously discussed Workers with Family Responsibilities Convention, 1981, are either exclusively or dominantly gender-neutral.

The gender-neutral focus rejects the concept of women as a separate class and emphasizes the idea of equal treatment between men and women. This does not mean, of course, that treaties with this focus do not make specific reference to women as a group; they do, but mostly insofar as they seek to end existing separation or special treatment.

Having stated the above, the convention included in this section suffers from a particular weakness—one which does not affect treaties of comparable importance. The committee which is authorized to monitor the progress states are making in implementing the convention's terms is limited to an annual two-week meeting period. Under no circumstances at all can the committee examine all the reports submitted by nation-states during the time allowed.

Convention on the Elimination of All Forms of Discrimination Against Women

[Adopted and opened for signature, ratification and accession by General Assembly resolution 34/180 of 18 December 1979]

Editor's Comments. *The General Assembly of the United Nations, by resolution 3521 (XXX) of December 15, 1975, requested the Commission on the Status of Women to complete, by 1976, the development and refinement of the then draft Convention on the Elimination of All Forms of Discrimination Against Women. That draft convention had been on the CSW agenda since 1970, and its adoption had been contemplated in the Program for U.N. Decade for Women (1976–1985) — a program which sought to focus on and effect improvement in the condition of women throughout the world. In step with the action required of it, the commission completed the draft convention in December 1976, and on December 18, 1979, by resolution 34/180 (XXXIV), the General Assembly adopted and opened for signature, ratification and accession the Convention on the Elimination of All Forms of Discrimination Against Women. Because, among other things, the adoption came during the U.N. Decade for Women, the General Assembly had expressed the hope that the convention, for symbolic and other reasons, would be signed and ratified without delay. That hope was realized. The convention, in accordance with Article 27 (1), came into force on September 3, 1981.*

The convention, which is the most comprehensive international instrument on women's rights, consists of thirty articles and is divided into a preamble and six parts. Part I (Articles 1–6) contains a number of general provisions; Part II (Articles 7–9) deals with matters relating to political rights; Part III (Articles 10–14) covers measures pertaining to social and economic rights; Part IV (Articles 15 and 16) includes provisions concerning civil and family rights; Part V (Articles 17–22) comprises measures respecting implementation; and Part VI (Articles 23–30) deals with what may be called principles which seek to improve the chances that the provisions of the Convention will be carried out. The full text follows.

The States Parties to the present Convention,

Noting that the Charter of the United Nations reaffirms faith in fundamental human rights, in the dignity and worth of the human person and in the equal rights of men and women,

Noting that the Universal Declaration of Human Rights affirms the principle of the inadmissibility of discrimination and proclaims that all human beings are born free and equal in dignity and rights and that everyone is entitled to all the rights and freedoms set forth therein, without distinction of any kind, including distinction based on sex,

Noting that the States Parties to the International Covenants on Human Rights have the obligation to ensure the equal right of men and women to enjoy all economic, social, cultural, civil and political rights,

Considering the international conventions concluded under the auspices of the United Nations and the specialized agencies promoting equality of rights of men and women,

Noting also the resolutions, declarations and recommendations adopted by the United Nations and the specialized agencies promoting equality of rights of men and women,

Concerned, however, that despite these various instruments extensive discrimination against women continues to exist,

Recalling that discrimination against women violates the principles of equality of rights and respect for human dignity, is an obstacle to the participation of women, on equal terms with men, in the political, social, economic and cultural life of their countries, hampers the growth of the prosperity of society and the family and makes more difficult the full development of the potentialities of women in the service of their countries and of humanity,

Concerned that in situations of poverty women have the least access to food, health, education, training and opportunities for employment and other needs,

Convinced that the establishment of the new international

economic order based on equity and justice will contribute significantly towards the promotion of equality between men and women,

Emphazing that the eradication of *apartheid*, all forms of racism, racial discrimination, colonialism, neo-colonialism, aggression, foreign occupation and domination and interference in the internal affairs of States is essential to the full enjoyment of the rights of men and women,

Affirming that the strengthening of international peace and security, the relaxation of international tension, mutual co-operation among all States irrespective of their social and economic systems, general and complete disarmament, in particular nuclear disarmament under strict and effective international control, the affirmation of the principles of justice, equality and mutual benefit in relations among countries and the realization of the right of peoples under alien and colonial domination and foreign occupation to self-determination and independence, as well as respect for national sovereignty and territorial integrity, will promote social progress and development and as a consequence will contribute to the attainment of full equality between men and women,

Convinced that the full and complete development of a country, the welfare of the world and the cause of peace require the maximum participation of women on equal terms with men in all fields,

Bearing in mind the great contribution of women to the welfare of the family and to the development of society, so far not fully recognized, the social significance of maternity and the role of both parents in the family and in the upbringing of children, and aware that the role of women in procreation should not be a basis for discrimination but that the upbringing of children requires a sharing of responsibility between men and women and society as a whole,

Aware that a change in the traditional role of men as well as the role of women in society and in the family is needed to achieve full equality between men and women,

Determined to implement the principles set forth in the Declaration on the Elimination of Discrimination Against Women and, for that purpose, to adopt the measures required for the elimination of such discrimination in all its forms and manifestations,

Have agreed on the following:

PART I

Article 1

For the purposes of the present Convention, the term "discrimination against women" shall mean any distinction, exclusion or restriction made on the basis of sex which has the effect or purpose of impairing or nullifying the recognition, enjoyment or exercise by women, irrespective of their marital status, on a basis of equality of men and women, of human rights and fundamental freedoms in the political, economic, social, cultural, civil or any other field.

Article 2

States Parties condemn discrimination against women in all its forms, agree to pursue by all appropriate means and without delay a policy of eliminating discrimination against women and, to this end, undertake:

(a) To embody the principle of the quality of men and women in their national constitutions or other appropriate legislation if not yet incorporated therein and to ensure, through law and other appropriate means, the practical realization of this principle;

(b) To adopt appropriate legislative and other measures, including sanctions where appropriate, prohibiting all discrimination against women;

(c) To establish legal protection of the rights of women on an equal basis with men and to ensure through competent national tribunals and other public institutions the effective protection of women against any act of discrimination;

(d) To refrain from engaging in any act or practice of discrimination against women and to ensure that public authorities and institutions shall act in conformity with this obligation;

(e) To take all appropriate measures to eliminate discrimination against women by any person, organization or enterprise;

(f) To take all appropriate measures, including legislation, to modify or abolish existing laws, regulations, customs and practices which constitute discrimination against women;

(g) To repeal all national penal provisions which constitute discrimination against women.

Article 3

States Parties shall take in all fields, in particular in the political, social, economic and cultural fields, all appropriate measures, including legislation, to ensure the full development and advancement of women, for the purpose of guaranteeing them the exercise and enjoyment of human rights and fundamental freedoms on a basis of equality with men.

Article 4

1. Adoption by States Parties of temporary special measures aimed at accelerating *de facto* equality between men and women shall not be considered discrimination as defined in the present Convention, but shall in no way entail as a consequence the maintenance of unequal or separate standards; these measures shall be discontinued when the objectives of equality of opportunity and treatment have been achieved.

2. Adoption by States Parties of special measures, including those measures contained in the present Convention, aimed at protecting maternity shall not be considered discriminatory.

Article 5

States Parties shall take all appropriate measures:

(a) To modify the social and cultural patterns of conduct of men and women, with a view to achieving the elimination of

prejudices and customary and all other practices which are based on the idea of the inferiority or the superiority of either of the sexes or on stereotyped roles for men and women;

(b) To ensure that family education includes a proper understanding of maternity as a social function and the recognition of the common responsibility of men and women in the upbringing and development of their children, it being understood that the interest of the children is the primordial consideration in all cases.

Article 6

States Parties shall take all appropriate measures including legislation, to suppress all forms of traffic in women and exploitation of prostitution of women.

PART II

Article 7

States Parties shall take all appropriate measures to eliminate discrimination against women in the political and public life of the country and, in particular, shall ensure to women, on equal terms with men, the right:

(a) To vote in all elections and public referenda and to be eligible for election to all publicly elected bodies;

(b) To participate in the formulation of government policy and the implementation thereof and to hold public office and perform all public functions at all levels of government;

(c) To participate in non-governmental organizations and associations concerned with the public and political life of the country.

Article 8

States Parties shall take all appropriate measures to ensure to women, on equal terms with men and without any discrimination, the opportunity to represent their Governments at the international level and to participate in the work of international organizations.

Article 9

1. States Parties shall grant women equal rights with men to acquire, change or retain their nationality. They shall ensure in particular that neither marriage to an alien nor change of nationality by the husband during marriage shall automatically change the nationality of the wife, render her stateless or force upon her the nationality of the husband.

2. States Parties shall grant women equal rights with men with respect to the nationality of their children.

PART III

Article 10

States Parties shall take all appropriate measures to eliminate discrimination against women in order to ensure to them equal rights with men in the field of educations and in particular to ensure, on a basis of equality of men and women:

(a) The same conditions for career and vocational guidance, for access to studies and for the achievement of diplomas in educational establishments of all categories in rural as well as in urban areas; this equality shall be ensured in pre-school, general, technical, professional and higher technical education, as well as in all types of vocational training;

(b) Access to the same curricula, the same examinations, teaching staff with qualifications of the same standard and school premises and equipment of the same quality;

(c) The elimination of any stereotyped concept of the roles of men and women at all levels and in all forms of educations by encouraging coeducation and other types of education which will help to achieve this aim and, in particular, by the revision of textbooks and school programmes and the adaptation of teaching methods;

(d) The same opportunities to benefit from scholarships and other study grants;

(e) The same opportunites for access to programmes of continuing education, including adult and functional literacy programmes, particularly those aimed at reducing at the earliest possible time, any gap in education existing between men and women;

(f) The reduction of female student drop-out rates and the organization of programmes for girls and women who have left school prematurely;

(g) The same opportunities to participate actively in sports and physical education;

(h) Access to specific educational information to help to ensure the health and well-being of families, including information and advice on family planning.

Article 11

1. States Parties shall take all appropriate measures to eliminate discrimination against women in the field of employment in order to ensure, on a basis of equality of men and women, the same rights, in particular:

(a) The right to work as an inalienable right of all human beings;

(b) The right to the same employment opportunities, including the application of the same criteria for selection in matters of employment;

(c) The right to free choice of profession and employment, the right to promotion, job security and all benefits and conditions of service and the right to receive vocational training and retraining, including apprenticeships, advanced vocational training and recurrent training;

(d) The right to equal remuneration, including benefits and to equal treatment in respect of work of equal value, as well as equality of treatment in the evaluation of the quality of work;

(*e*) The right to social security; particularly in cases of retirement, unemployment, sickness, invalidity and old age and other incapacity to work, as well as the right to paid leave;

(*f*) The right to protection of health and to safety in working conditions, including the safeguarding of the function of reproduction.

2. In order to prevent discrimination against women on the grounds of marriage or maternity and to ensure their effective right to work, States Parties shall take appropriate measures:

(*a*) To prohibit, subject to the imposition of sanctions, dismissal on the grounds of pregnancy or of maternity leave and discrimination in dismissals on the basis of marital status;

(*b*) To introduce maternity leave with pay or with comparable social benefits without loss of former employment, seniority or social allowances;

(*c*) To encourage the provision of the necessary supporting social services to enable parents to combine family obligations with work responsibilities and participation in public life, in particular through promoting the establishment and development of a network of child-care facilities;

(*d*) To provide special protection to women during pregnancy in types of work proved to be harmful to them.

3. Protective legislation relating to matters covered in this article shall be reviewed periodically in the light of scientific and technological knowledge and shall be revised, repealed or extended as necessary.

Article 12

1. States Parties shall take all appropriate measures to eliminate discrimination against women in the field of health care in order to ensure, on a basis of equality of men and women, access to health care services, including those related to family planning.

2. Notwithstanding the provisions of paragraph 1 of this

Article, States Parties shall ensure to women appropriate services in connexion with pregnancy, confinement and the postnatal period, granting free services where necessary, as well as adequate nutrition during pregnancy and lactation.

Article 13

States Parties shall take all appropriate measures to eliminate discrimination against women in other areas of economic and social life in order to ensure, on a basis of equality of men and women, the same rights, in particular:

(a) The right to family benefits;

(b) The right to bank loans, mortgages and other forms of financial credit;

(c) The right to participate in recreational activities, sports and all aspects of cultural life.

Article 14

1. States Parties shall take into account the particular problems faced by rural women and the significant roles which rural women play in the economic survival of their families, including their work in the non-monetized sectors of the economy, and shall take all appropriate measures to ensure the application of the provisions of the present Convention to women in rural areas.

2. States Parties shall take all appropriate measures to eliminate discrimination against women in rural areas in order to ensure, on a basis of equality of men and women, that they participate in and benefit from rural development and, in particular, shall ensure to such women the right:

(a) To participate in the elaboration and implementation of development planning at all levels;

(b) To have access to adequate health care facilities, including information, counselling and services in family planning;

(c) To benefit directly from social security programmes;

(d) To obtain all types of training and education, formal and

non-formal, including that relating to functional literacy, as well as *inter alia,* the benefit of all community and extension services, in order to increase their technical proficiency;

(e) To organize self-help groups and co-operatives in order to obtain equal access to economic opportunities through employment or self-employment;

(f) To participate in all community activities;

(g) To have access to agricultural credit and loans, marketing facilities, appropriate technology and equal treatment in land and agrarian reform as well as in land resettlement schemes;

(h) To enjoy adequate living conditions, particularly in relation to housing, sanitation, electricity and water supply, transport and communications.

PART IV

Article 15

1. States Parties shall accord to women equality with men before the law.

2. States Parties shall accord to women, in civil matters, a legal capacity identical to that of men and the same opportunities to exercise that capacity. In particular, they shall give women equal rights to conclude contracts and to administer property and shall treat them equally in all stages of procedure in courts and tribunals.

3. States Parties agree that all contracts and all other private instruments of any kind with a legal effect which is directed at restricting the legal capacity of women shall be deemed null and void.

4. States Parties shall accord to men and women the same rights with regard to the law relating to the movement of persons and the freedom to choose their residence and domicile.

Article 16

1. States Parties shall take all appropriate measures to

eliminate discrimination against women in all matters relating to marriage and family relations and in particular shall ensure, on a basis of equality of men and women:

(a) The same right to enter into marriage;

(b) The same right freely to choose a spouse and to enter into marriage only with their free and full consent;

(c) The same rights and responsibilities during marriage and at its dissolution;

(d) The same rights and responsibilities as parents, irrespective of their marital status, in matters relating to their children; in all cases the interests of the children shall be paramount;

(e) The same rights to decide freely and responsibly on the number and spacing of their children and to have access to the information, education and means to enable them to exercise these rights;

(f) The same rights and responsibilities with regard to guardianship, wardship, trusteeship and adoption of children, or similiar institutions where these concepts exist in national legislation; in all cases the interests of the children shall be paramount;

(g) The same personal rights as husband and wife, including the right to choose a family name, a profession and an occupation;

(h) The same rights for both spouses in respect of the ownership, acquisition, management, administration, enjoyment and disposition of property, whether free of charge or for a valuable consideration.

2. The betrothal and the marriage of a child shall have no legal effect, and all necessary action, including legislation, shall be taken to specify a minimum age for marriage and to make the registration of marriages in an official registry compulsory.

PART V

Article 17

1. For the purposes of considering the progress made in the

implementation of the present Convention, there shall be established a Committee on the Elimination of Discrimination Against Women (hereinafter referred to as the Committee) consisting, at the time of entry into force of the Convention, of eighteen and after ratification of or accession to the Convention by the thirty-fifth State Party, of twenty-three experts of high moral standing and competence in the field covered by the Convention. The experts shall be elected by States Parties from among their nationals and shall serve in their personal capacity, consideration being given to equitable geographical distribution and to the representation of the different forms of civilization as well as the principal legal systems.

2. The members of the Committee shall be elected by secret ballot from a list of persons nominated by States Parties. Each State Party may nominate one person from among its own nationals.

3. The initial election shall be held six months after the date of the entry into force of the present Convention. At least three months before the date of each election the Secretary-General of the United Nations shall address a letter to the States Parties inviting them to submit their nominations within two months. The Secretary-General shall prepare a list in alphabetical order of all persons thus nominated, indicating the States Parties which have nominated them, and shall submit it to the States Parties.

4. Elections of the members of the Committee shall be held at a meeting of States Parties convened by the Secretary-General at United Nations Headquarters. At that meeting, for which two-thirds of the States Parties shall constitute a quorum, the persons elected to the Committee shall be those nominees who obtain the largest number of votes and an absolute majority of the votes of the representatives of States Parties present and voting.

5. The members of the Committee shall be elected for a term of four years. However, the terms of nine of the members elected at the first election shall expire at the end of two years; immediately after the first election the names of these nine members shall be chosen by lot by the Chairman of the Committee.

6. The election of the five additional members of the Committee shall be held in accordance with the provisions of paragraphs 2, 3, and 4 of this Article, following the thirty-fifth ratification or accession. The terms of two of the additional members elected on this occasion shall expire at the end of two years, the names of these two members having been chosen by lot by the Chairman of the Committee.

7. For the filling of casual vacancies, the State Party whose expert has ceased to function as a member of the Committee shall appoint another expert from among its nationals, subject to the approval of the Committee.

8. The members of the Committee shall, with the approval of the General Assembly, receive emoluments from United Nations resources on such terms and conditions as the Assembly may decide, having regard to the importance of the Committee's responsibilities.

9. The Secretary-General of the United Nations shall provide the necessary staff and facilities for the effective performance of the functions of the Committee under the present Convention.

Article 18

1. States Parties undertake to submit to the Secretary-General of the United Nations, for consideration by the Committee, a report on the legislative, judicial, administrative or other measures which they have adopted to give effect to the provisions of the present Convention and on the progress made in this respect:

(a) Within one year after the entry into force for the State concerned;

(b) Thereafter at least every four years and further whenever the Committee so requests.

2. Reports may indicate factors and difficulties affecting the degree of fulfilment of obligations under the present Convention.

Article 19

1. The Committee shall adopt its own rules of procedure.

2. The Committee shall elect its officers for a term of two years.

Article 20

1. The Committee shall normally meet for a period of not more than two weeks annually in order to consider the reports submitted in accordance with Article 18 of the present Convention.

2. The meetings of the Committee shall normally be held at United Nations Headquarters or at any other convenient place as determined by the Committee.

Article 21

1. The Committee shall, through the Economic and Social Council, report annually to the General Assembly of the United Nations on its activities and may make suggestions and general recommendations based on the examination of reports and information received from the States Parties. Such suggestions and general recommendations shall be included in the report of the Committee together with comments, if any, from States Parties.

2. The Secretary-General of the United Nations shall transmit the reports of the Committee to the Commission on the Status of Women for its information.

Article 22

The specialized agencies shall be entitled to be represented at the consideration of the implementation of such provisions of the present Convention as fall within the scope of their activities. The Committee may invite the specialized agencies to submit reports on the implementation of the Convention in areas falling within the scope of their activities.

Part VI

Article 23

Nothing in the present Convention shall affect any provisions that are more conducive to the achievement of equality between men and women which may be contained:

(a) In the legislation of a State Party; or

(b) In any other international convention, treaty or agreement in force for that State.

Article 24

States parties undertake to adopt all necessary measures at the national level aimed at achieving the full realization of the rights recognized in the present Convention.

Article 25

1. The present Convention shall be open for signature by all States.

2. The Secretary-General of the United Nations is designated as the depositary of the present Convention.

3. The present Convention is subject to ratification. Instruments of ratification shall be deposited with the Secretary-General of the United Nations.

4. The present Convention shall be open to accession by all States. Accession shall be effected by the deposit of an instrument of accession with the Secretary-General of the United Nations.

Article 26

1. A request for the revision of the present Convention may be made at any time by any State Party by means of a notification in writing addressed to the Secretary-General of the United Nations.

2. The General Assembly of the United Nations shall

decide upon the steps, if any, to be taken in respect of such a request.

Article 27

1. The present Convention shall enter into force on the thirtieth day after the date of deposit with the Secretary-General of the United Nations of the twentieth instrument of ratification or accession.

2. For each State ratifying the present Convention or acceding to it after the deposit of the twentieth instrument of ratification or accession, the Convention shall enter into force on the thirtieth day after the date of the deposit of its own instrument of ratification or accession.

Article 28

1. The Secretary-General of the United Nations shall receive and circulate to all States the text of reservations made by States at the time of ratification or accession.

2. A reservation incompatible with the object and purpose of the present Convention shall not be permitted.

3. Reservations may be withdrawn at any time by notification to this effect addressed to the Secretary-General of the United Nations, who shall then inform all States thereof. Such notification shall take effect on the date on which it is received.

Article 29

1. Any dispute between two or more States Parties concerning the interpretation or application of the present Convention which is not settled by negotiation shall, at the request of one of them, be submitted to arbitration. If within six months from the date of the request for arbitration the parties are unable to agree on the organization of the arbitration, any one of those parties may refer the dispute to the International Court of Justice by request in conformity with the Statute of the Court.

2. Each State Party may at the time of signature or ratifica-

tion of the present Convention or accession thereto declare that it does not consider itself bound by paragraph 1 of this Article. The other States Parties shall not be bound by that paragraph with respect to any State Party which has made such a reservation.

3. Any State Party which has made a reservation in accordance with paragraph 2 of this Article may at any time withdraw that reservation by notification to the Secretary-General of the United Nations.

Article 30

The present Convention, the Arabic, Chinese, English, French, Russian and Spanish texts of which are equally authentic, shall be deposited with the Secretary-General of the United Nations.

In witness whereof the undersigned, duly authorized, have signed the present Convention.

Declaration on the Elimination of Discrimination Against Women

[Proclaimed by the General Assembly resolution 2263(XXII) of 7 November 1967]

The General Assembly,

Considering that the peoples of the United Nations have, in the Charter, reaffirmed their faith in fundamental human rights, in the dignity and worth of the human person and in the equal rights of men and women,

Considering that the Universal Declaration on Human Rights asserts the principle of non-discrimination and proclaims that all human beings are born free and equal in dignity and rights and that everyone is entitled to all the rights and freedoms set forth therein, without distinction of any kind, including any distinction as to sex,

Taking into account the resolutions, declarations, conventions and recommendations of the United Nations and the specialized agencies designed to eliminate all forms of discrimination and to promote equal rights for men and women,

Concerned that, despite the Charter of the United Nations, the Universal Declaration of Human Rights, the International Covenants on Human Rights and other instruments of the United Nations and the specialized agencies and despite the progress made in the matter of equality of rights, there continues to exist considerable discrimination against women,

Considering that discrimination against women is incompatible with human dignity and with the welfare of the family and of society, prevents their participation, on equal terms with men, in the political, social, economic and cultural life of their countries and is an obstacle to the full development of the potentialities of women in the service of their countries and of humanity,

Bearing in mind the great contribution made by women to

social, political, economic and cultural life and the part they play in the family and particularly in the rearing of children,

Convinced that the full and complete development of a country, the welfare of the world and the cause of peace require the maximum participation of women as well as men in all fields,

Considering that it is necessary to ensure the universal recognition in law and in fact of the principle of equality of men and women,

Solemnly proclaims this Declaration:

Article 1

Discrimination against women, denying or limiting as it does their equality of rights with men, is fundamentally unjust and constitutes an offence against human dignity.

Article 2

All appropriate measures shall be taken to abolish existing laws, customs, regulations and practices which are discriminatory against women, and to establish adequate legal protection for equal rights of men and women, in particular:

(a) The principle of equality of rights shall be embodied in the constitution or otherwise guaranteed by law;

(b) The international instruments of the United Nations and the specialized agencies relating to the elimination of discrimination against women shall be ratified or acceded to and fully implemented as soon as practicable.

Article 3

All appropriate measures shall be taken to educate public opinion and to direct national aspirations towards the eradication of prejudice and the abolition of customary and all other practices which are based on the idea of the inferiority of women.

Article 4

All appropriate measures shall be taken to ensure to women on equal terms with men, without any discrimination:

(a) The right to vote in all elections and be eligible for election to all publicly elected bodies;

(b) The right to vote in all public referenda;

(c) The right to hold public office and to exercise all public functions.

Such rights shall be guaranteed by legislation.

Article 5

Women shall have the same rights as men to acquire, change or retain their nationality. Marriage to an alien shall not automatically affect the nationality of the wife either by rendering her stateless or by forcing upon her the nationality of her husband.

Article 6

1. Without prejudice to the safeguarding of the unity and the harmony of the family, which remains the basic unit of any society, all appropriate measures, particularly legislative measures, shall be taken to ensure to women, married or unmarried, equal rights with men in the field of civil law, and in particular:

(a) The right to acquire, administer, enjoy, dispose of and inherit property, including property acquired during marriage;

(b) The right to equality in legal capacity and the exercise thereof;

(c) The same rights as men with regard to the law on the movement of persons.

2. All appropriate measures shall be taken to ensure the principle of equality of status of the husband and wife, and in particular:

(a) Women shall have the same right as men to free choice of a spouse and to enter into marriage only with their free and full consent;

(b) Women shall have equal rights with men during marriage and at its dissolution. In all cases the interest of the children shall be paramount;

(c) Parents shall have equal rights and duties in matters relating to their children. In all cases the interest of the children shall be paramount.

3. Child marriage and the betrothal of young girls before puberty shall be prohibited, and effective action, including legislation, shall be taken to specify a minimum age for marriage and to make the registration of marriages in an official registry compulsory.

Article 7

All provisions of penal codes which constitute discrimination against women shall be repealed.

Article 8

All appropriate measures, including legislation, shall be taken to combat all forms of traffic in women and exploitation of prostitution of women.

Article 9

All appropriate measures shall be taken to ensure to girls and women, married or unmarried, equal rights with men in education at all levels, and in particular:

(a) Equal conditions of access to, and study in, educational institutions of all types, including universities and vocational, technical and professional schools;

(b) The same choice of curricula, the same examinations, teaching staff with qualifications of the same standard, and school premises and equipment of the same quality, whether the institutions are co-educational or not;

(c) Equal opportunities to benefit from scholarships and other study grants;

(d) Equal opportunities for access to programmes of continuing education, including adult literacy programmes;

(e) Access to educational information to help in ensuring the health and well-being of families.

Article 10

1. All appropriate measures shall be taken to ensure to women, married or unmarried, equal rights with men in the field of economic and social life, and in particular:

(a) The right, without discrimination on grounds of marital status or any other grounds, to receive vocational training, to work, to free choice of profession and employment, and to professional and vocational advancement;

(b) The right to equal remuneration with men and to equality of treatment in respect of work of equal value;

(c) The right to leave with pay, retirement privileges and provision for security in respect of unemployment, sickness, old age or other incapacity to work;

(d) The right to receive family allowances on equal terms with men.

2. In order to prevent discrimination against women on account of marriage or maternity and to ensure their effective right to work, measures shall be taken to prevent their dismissal in the event of marriage or maternity and to provide paid maternity leave, with the guarantee of returning to former employment, and to provide the necessary social services, including childcare facilities.

3. Measures taken to protect women in certain types of work, for reasons inherent in their physical nature, shall not be regarded as discriminatory.

Article 11

1. The principle of equality of rights of men and women

demands implementation in all States in accordance with the principles of the Charter of the United Nations and of the Universal Declaration of Human Rights.

2. Governments, non-governmental organizations and individuals are urged, therefore, to do all in their power to promote the implementation of the principles contained in this Declaration.

Appendix A

Two Regional Conventions

Convention on the Nationality of Women

Convention signed at Montevideo December 26, 1933
Senate advice and consent to ratification May 24, 1934
Ratified by the President of the United States June 30, 1934
Ratification of the United States deposited with the Pan
    American Union July 13, 1934
Entered into force August 29, 1934
Proclaimed by the President of the United States
    October 11, 1934

49 Statute 2957; Treaty Series 875

The Governments represented in the Seventh International Conference of American States:

Who, after having exhibited their Full Powers, which were found in good and due form, have agreed upon the following:

Article 1

There shall be no distinction based on sex as regards nationality, in their legislation or in their practice.

Article 2

The present convention shall be ratified by the High Contracting Parties in conformity with their respective constitutional procedures. The Minister of Foreign Affairs of the Republic of Uruguay shall transmit authentic certified copies to the governments for the aforementioned purpose of ratification. The instrument of ratification shall be deposited in the archives of the Pan American Union in Washington, which shall notify the signatory governments of said deposit. Such notification shall be considered as an exchange of ratifications.

Article 3

The present convention will enter into force between the High Contracting Parties in the order in which they deposit their respective ratifications.

Article 4

The present convention shall remain in force indefinitely but may be denounced by means of one year's notice given to the Pan American Union, which shall transmit it to the other signatory governments. After the expiration of this period the convention shall cease in its effects as regards the party which denounces but shall remain in effect for the remaining High Contracting Parties.

Article 5

The present convention shall be open for adherence and accession of the States which are not signatories. The corresponding instruments shall be deposited in the archives of the Pan American Union which shall communicate them to the other High Contracting Parties.

In witness whereof, the following Plenipotentiaries have signed this convention in Spanish, English, Portuguese and French and hereunto affix their respective seals in the city of Montevideo, Republic of Uruguay, this 26th day of December, 1933.

Inter-American Convention on the Granting of Political Rights to Women

[27 U.S.T. 3301; T.I.A.S. No. 8365]

The Governments Represented at the Ninth International Conference of American States,

Considering:

That the majority of the American Republics, inspired by lofty principles of justice, have granted political rights to women;

That it has been a constant aspiration of the American community of nations to equalize the status of men and women in the enjoyment and exercise of political rights;

That Resolution XX of the Eighth International Conference of American States expressly declares:
   "That women have the right to political treatment on the basis of equality with men";

That long before the women of America demanded their rights they were able to carry out nobly all their responsibilities side by side with men;

That the principle of equality of human rights for men and women is contained in the Charter of the United Nations,

Have resolved:

To authorize their respective Representatives, whose Full Powers have been found to be in good and due form, to sign the following articles:

Article 1

The High Contracting Parties agree that the right to vote and to be elected to national office shall not be denied or abridged by reason of sex.

Article 2

The present Convention shall be open for signature by the American States and shall be ratified in accordance with their constitutional procedures. The original instrument, the English, French, Portuguese and Spanish tests of which are equally authentic, shall be deposited with the General Secretariat of the Organization of American States, which shall transmit certified copies to the Governments for the purpose of ratification. The instruments of ratification shall be deposited with the General Secretariat of the Organization of American States, which shall notify the signatory Governments of the said deposit. Such notification shall serve as an exchange of ratifications.

Reservations

Reservation of the Delegation of Honduras.

The Delegation of Honduras makes a reservation with respect to the granting of political rights to women, in view of the fact that the political Constitution of its country grants the prerogatives of citizenship to men only.

Declaration of the Delegation of Mexico.

The Mexican Delegation, in expressing its appreciation of the spirit that inspires the present Convention, declares that it abstains from signing it inasmuch as, according to Article 2, the Convention is open to signature by the American States. The Government of Mexico reserves the right to adhere to the Convention when, taking into consideration existing constitutional provisions of Mexico, it considers such adherence appropriate.

Appendix B

Selected List of Other Conventions Relating to Women

Convention Concerning the Employment of Women During the Night. (Adopted by the ILO, November 29, 1919, and modified in 1946.) Vol. 38 U.N.T.S., p. 67.

Convention Concerning Compulsory Widows' and Orphans' Insurance for Persons Employed in Industrial or Commercial Undertakings, in the Liberal Professions and for Outworkers and Domestic Servants. (Adopted June 29, 1933, and modified in 1946.) Vol. 39 U.N.T.S., p. 259.

Convention Concerning the Employment of Women During the Night. (Adopted by the ILO, June 19, 1934, and modified in 1946.) Vol. 40 U.N.T.S., p. 3.

Convention Concerning the Employment of Women on Underground Work in Mines of All Kinds. (Adopted by the ILO, June 21, 1935, and modified in 1946.) Vol. 40 U.N.T.S., p. 63.

Convention Concerning Night Work of Women Employed in Industry. (Adopted by the ILO, July 9, 1948.) Vol. 81 U.N.T.S., p. 147.

Convention Concerning Minimum Standards of Social Security. (Adopted by the ILO, June 28, 1952.) Vol. 210 U.N.T.S., p. 131.

Convention Concerning Conditions of Employment of Plantation Workers. (Adopted by the ILO, June 24, 1958.) Vol. 348 U.N.T.S., p. 275.

Notes

Introduction

1. League of Nations, *League of Nations Treaty Series,* CLXXXIX No. 4137, p. 89.
2. See Art. 11 of the Covenant on the Elimination of All Forms of Discrimination Against Women (CEDAW) in Vol. 34 U.N. GAOR Supp. (No. 46), U.N. Doc. A/34180 (1980).
3. *Ibid.* See also Art. 25 of the Universal Declaration of Human Rights (UNDHR) which states that "motherhood and childhood are entitled to special care and assistance."
4. See Art. 13 of CEDAW.
5. United Nations, *The United Nations in the Field of Human Rights* ST/HR/2 Rev. 2 (1983).
6. United Nations, *Report of the World Conference to Review and Appraise the Achievements of the United Naitons Decade for Women: Equality, Development and Peace* (Nairobi, 15-26 July 1985) A/CONF. 116/28 Rev.1.
7. Quoted in Burns H. Weston, Richard Falk, and Anthony A. D'Amato. *International Law and World Order* (St. Paul, Minn: West Publishing Co., 1980), pp. 578–580.
8. *Ibid.*

I. The U.N. Charter and the International Bill of Rights

1. See the preamble of the UDHR.
2. *Ibid.*
3. See memorandum of the Office of Legal Affairs, United Nations Secretariat Vol. 34 U.N. ESCOR, Supp. (no. 8) 15 U.N. Doc. E/CN. 4/1/610 (1962).
4. Louis Henkin, (ed.), *The International Bill of Rights* (New York: Columbia University Press, 1981), p. 10.
5. See GAOR 3rd Sess. Part I, 3rd Committee, 95th Meeting (Wednesday, Oct. 6, 1948), p. 92.

6. *Ibid.*, p. 558.

II. Employment, Remuneration and Education

1. See the preamble of the ILO's constitution.

2. See Art. 1 of UNESCO's constitution.

3. This is the name by which the ILO itself says the treaty may be cited.

4. See Art. 1 of the Convention.

5. This convention may be found in Vol. 38 U.N.T.S., p. 53.

6. See Art. 1 (a) of the 1919 Convention and of its 1952 successor to observe the difference.

7. Some of these provisions are to be found in the 1958 Convention Concerning Conditions of Employment of Plantation Workers adopted by the General Conference of the ILO June 24, 1958. Vol. 348 U.N.T.S., p. 275.

8. See Art. 8 of the European Social Charter. That Charter was adopted on October 18, 1961 and came into force February 26, 1965. *Europ. T.S.* No. 35.

9. The Convention Concerning Employment Policy, adopted by the ILO on July 9, 1964, is also important in some respects. It aims to assure, *inter alia,* that "there is freedom of choice of employment and the fullest opportunity for each worker to qualify for, and to use his skills and endowments in a job for which he is well suited, irrespective of . . . sex . . . ." See Art. 1(c) at Vol. 569 U.N.T.S., p. 32.

10. An example of such special measures is the Convention on Maternity Protection.

11. See Art. 26 of the UDHR; see also the preamble of the Convention Against Discrimination in Education at Vol. 429 U.N.T.S., p. 93.

12. See Art. 1(1) of the Convention under discussion.

13. See *Study of the Inter-Relationship of the Status of Women and Family Planning* (Report of the Special Rapporteur) 13, U.N. Doc. E/CN. 6/575 (1973).

14. Alison Bass, "Studies Find Workplace Still a Man's World" *Boston Globe* (March 12, 1990).

III. Nationality

1. There are certain limited protections available under the human rights regime.

2. Sovereignty plays a role here, also.

3. Exceptions are made for the children of diplomats, foreign heads of state, and consular officials.

4. See Art. 15 of the UDHR. For further readings on the issue of the nationality of women see U.N. *Conventions on the Nationality of Married Women: Historical Background and Commentary Vol. 25 U.N. Doc. E/CN.*

6/389 (1962); United Nations, *Nationality of Married Women* U.N. Doc.
E/CN. 6/254/Rev.1 (1963).

IV. Marriage, Family and Children

1. The writer does not overlook marriages between the same gender,
but takes the view that tradition rarely recognizes this type of marriage.

2. *Hearings on Equal Rights for Men and Women 1971 Before Subcom-
mittee No. 4 of the House Committee on the Judiciary*, 92nd Cong., 1'st Session, ser 2, #106, 108, 369–400 (1975).

3. Cynthia Enloe, *Making Feminist Sense of International Politics*
(Berkeley: University of California Press, 1989), Chap. 5.

4. See Final Act of the United Nations Conference of Plenepoten-
tiaries on a Supplemental Convention of the Abolition of Slavery, the
Slave Trade, and Institutions and Practices Similar to Slavery in Vol. 266
U.N.T.S., p. 3.

5. See Convention Relative to the Protection of Civilian Persons in
Time of War Vol. 75 U.N.T.S., p. 287.

6. See UNGA Doc. A/7720 (November 20, 1969) and UNGA Doc.
A/8052 (September 18, 1970); Richard R. Baxter, "Humanitarian Law
or Humanitarian Politics? The 1974 Diplomatic Conference on
Humanitarian Law" in *Harvard Int. Law Journal* Vol. XVI (1975), pp.
1–26; Geoffrey Best, *Humanity in Warfare* (New York: Columbia
University Press, 1980).

7. These were adopted by consensus in 1977, after thorough discussion by the Diplomatic Conference on Reaffirmation and Development
of International Humanitarian Law Applicable to Armed Conflict
1974–1977. See Baxter, *op. cit.*, Note 7.

8. See Art. 1 of the following declaration.

9. See Part Two of this volume.

10. See paragraph 14 of the preamble of the Convention of the
Elimination of all Forms of Discrimination Against Women.

11. See Art. 1 (2) and (3) in Workers with Family Responsibilities
Convention.

12. There are differences in the capacity of certain states, Third World
countries for example, to implement the terms of the treaty.

13. See Art. 7.

14. See Art. 8.

V. Prostitution and Slavery

1. See *Report of Mr. Jean Fernand-Laurent, Special Rapporteur on the
suppression of the traffic in persons and the exploitation of the prostitution of
others.* Delivered to the First Regular Session of the Economic and Social
Council of 1983, No. 12 of the Provisional Agenda. (Activities for the Advancement of Women, Equality, Development and Peace) U.N. Doc.

E/1983/7 (March 17, 1983). See also Kathleen Barry, Charlotte Bunch, and Shirley Castley (eds.), *International Feminism: Networking Against Female Sexual Slavery* (Report of the Global Feminist Workshop to Organize Against Traffic in Women, Rottendom, the Netherlands, April 6–15, 1983).

    2. See Art. 1 of Convention, which may be found at Vol. 96 U.N.T.S., p. 271.

    3. See Arts. 2 & 3.

    4. See Arts. 8, 15, 16, 19.

VI. Political Rights

    1. See discussion of the Third Committee of the General Assembly (478th and 479th meetings, for example), U.N. GAOR (Seventh Session), 1952 U.N. Doc. A/c.3/SR.478 & 479.

    2. *Ibid.,* p. 375.

    3. See the *New York Times* (January 6, 1990) p. 14.

    4. Ruth L. Sivard, *Women . . . A World Survey* (Washington D.C.: World Priorities, 1985), p. 35.

    5. United Nations *United Nations Actions in the Field of Human Rights* ST/HR/2 Rev.2, p. 88.

    6. See *Report of World Conference, op. cit.,* note 6 in Introduction.

VII. All Discrimination

    1. Adopted June 21, 1935. Vol. 40 U.N.T.S., p. 63.

    2. *Ibid.,* Art. 2.

    3. Natalie K. Heavener, "An Analysis of Gender Based Treaty Law: Contemporary Developments in Historical Perspective" in *Human Rights Quarterly* Vol. VIII #1 (February, 1986), pp. 71–72.

Index